Much More Than Counting

More Math Activities for Preschool and Kindergarten

by
Sally Moomaw
and
Brenda Hieronymus

Redleaf Press

Published by: Redleaf Press
                 a division of Resources for Child Caring, Inc.
                 450 North Syndicate, Suite 5
                 St. Paul, MN 55104-4125

Distributed by: Gryphon House
                 Mailing Address:
                 P.O. Box 207
                 Beltsville, MD 20704-0207

Library of Congress Cataloging-in-Publication Data

Moomaw, Sally, 1948-
    Much more than counting: more math activities for preschool and
kindergarten / by Sally Moomaw and Brenda Hieronymus.
        p.   cm.
    Includes bibliographical references.
    ISBN 1-884834-66-3
    1. Mathematics—Study and teaching (Preschool) 2. Mathematics —
Study and teaching —Activity programs. I. Hieronymus, Brenda, 1945-
II. Title. III. Title: More than counting
    QA135.5 .M6154 1999
    372.7 — dc21   99-31622
                                                          CIP

table support children's construction of math concepts, important opportunities for mathematical thinking and problem solving occur throughout the day. Teachers need to plan for and capitalize on these situations.

Teachers' Questions

Why is it important to include math activities throughout the classroom?

Each area of the classroom presents unique possibilities for children to encounter real math problems to solve through their play. From dividing eggs equitably in the dramatic play area to finding enough triangular-shaped blocks for the entire perimeter of the roof of a block structure, children must deal with real-life math issues throughout their day. Teachers can increase the possibilities for children to engage in mathematical thinking by imbedding opportunities for mathematical reasoning in their plans for each area of the classroom. This increases the opportunities for all children to stretch their mathematical thinking throughout the day.

What areas of the classroom provide the best opportunities for children to engage in mathematical thinking?

All areas of the classroom have exciting math potential. The activities included in this chapter offer suggestions for incorporating math concepts into the dramatic play, block, manipulative, sensory, art, and music areas of the classroom. Math opportunities during gross-motor play and snack time are also included.

Why do some children avoid math materials?

Children may avoid traditional math materials because they find them boring. Teachers can confront this problem by presenting mathematical concepts through a game format. Children find math games to be challenging and exciting, and they often play them over and over again. Ideas for developing math games are presented in chapters 5, 6, and 7 of this book and in our previous book, *More Than Counting*.

A few children may avoid even the most inviting math materials because they feel insecure in the math area or fear failure. Classrooms, recreational programs, or families where adults correct children for errors in counting or quantifying may unintentionally foster such feelings of inadequacy. Teachers should maintain an atmosphere in the classroom that encourages children to explore math concepts. Adults working with children can be reminded that errors are evidence of a child's current level of thinking rather than mistakes that need to be corrected.

Math Throughout the Classroom

Ian seemed to be lagging in the formation of basic math concepts, such as one-to-one correspondence. He showed little sustained interest in math materials. His teaching team discussed their concerns and decided that they needed to take math to Ian rather than continuing to take Ian to math. Since Ian liked dramatic play, his teachers decided to plan specific one-to-one correspondence activities for that area. They used colored tape to divide a cookie sheet into boxes and introduced cookie magnets that fit into the boxes. Ian was very attracted to the new materials. Soon he was carefully placing one cookie magnet into each box on the cookie sheet. Shortly thereafter, he began using one-to-one correspondence to play math games.

▲ ▲ ▲

A crowd of children gathered every day in the farmers' market in the dramatic play area. The large basket of fruits and vegetables was constantly dumped on the floor. The teacher was disappointed in the quality of play in the center. Her director suggested that individual baskets for each type of food might alleviate the dumping problem. After the teacher made this small change, she noticed an entirely different type of play emerging. Children started sorting the food into categories. They began counting how many they had of each type of food and comparing the quantities. Some children attempted to apportion the foods so that each child had the same amount. The teacher was delighted. "Now I'm seeing math relationships emerge in the children's play," she told the director.

▲ ▲ ▲

Math skills emerge as children encounter situations that encourage mathematical thinking. The National Council of Teachers of Mathematics "see classrooms as places where interesting problems are regularly explored using important mathematical ideas."[1] While math materials on the manipulative shelves or a math game

suggestions for modifying each activity to make it more complex or less difficult. In this way, teachers can design activities to best meet the needs of individual children or their group.

Throughout this book, reference is made to teachers and their role in guiding young children in the construction of mathematical knowledge. The term *teachers* is meant to be inclusive. All those who work with young children are teachers, whether they are parents, child care workers, or classroom aides. This book is designed to meet the needs of a wide spectrum of people who care for and nurture young children.

With the exception of the chapter for toddlers, the activities in this book were designed for preschool and kindergarten children, age three and older. Some of the materials contain small pieces. If teachers have children who still put things into their mouths, they should be certain to use pieces that young children cannot swallow.

All of the activities that appear in *Much More Than Counting* have been field-tested in classrooms at the Arlitt Child and Family Research and Education Center at the University of Cincinnati. The children at the center come from diverse family backgrounds. Some are funded by Head Start, some pay tuition, and others are funded through an agency for children with disabilities. The children represent many different cultures and nationalities and speak many different languages, yet all experience the excitement of exploring math throughout the classroom.

Teachers and parents share in the enthusiasm of young children as they learn to solve problems, discover and create patterns and relationships, and communicate their findings. It is our hope that this book will continue the process of helping children explore the many features of math that we initially described in *More Than Counting*.

mathematical knowledge at this crucial period of development. Chapter 4 provides specific suggestions for how to assemble and display traditional toddler materials to increase their math potential. It also gives ideas for comments and questions to encourage mathematical development for toddlers.

Math manipulative materials enable children to solve problems using concrete, movable objects. When interesting counters are combined with a die or spinner, children naturally begin to create and compare sets and quantify. Chapter 5 includes a wide variety of math manipulative activities that coordinate with popular curriculum topics. These activities invite children to explore mathematical concepts as they manipulate the materials and discuss the results.

Carefully designed board games span a range of stages of mathematical thinking in young children. From grid games, which are typically the easiest, to short and long path games, which increase in difficulty, board games encourage children to stretch their mathematical thinking and move forward in their problem-solving and quantification skills. When math games coordinate with other areas of the curriculum, such as a favorite book or an exciting dramatic play area design, children are especially motivated to play them. For this reason, the grid and board games in chapters 6 and 7 are linked to popular curriculum topics. The grid games in chapter 6 are paired with short and long path games in chapter 7 so that children on many different levels can successfully play math games related to a favorite topic. Chapter 7 includes many more complex path games for kindergarten children as well as less difficult games for younger or less-experienced children.

Many early childhood classrooms are inclusive environments in which children with specific disabilities fully participate with typically developing children. Children with disabilities enjoy and benefit from the same curriculum materials as typically developing children. Simple modifications can make specific activities accessible to all children. Chapter 8 contains suggestions for adapting math activities for children with disabilities in cognitive, motor, language, visual, and hearing development.

Mathematical thinking does not occur in isolation from other areas of learning. For this reason, each activity in *Much More Than Counting* contains ideas for integrated curriculum activities. Since teachers have reported to us that they often like to coordinate activities from the other books in this curriculum series, many of the integrated curriculum sections refer readers to specific activities in the other books in the series published by Redleaf Press: *More Than Counting* (1995), *More Than Singing* (1997), *More Than Magnets* (1997), and *More Than Painting* (1999). There are also

Preface

Since the release of *More Than Counting* four years ago, we have continued to present workshops to teachers around the country. Teachers have enthusiastically told us that they want *much more*—more math manipulatives, more grid games, and more path games. We have also received many requests to include material about toddlers, children with disabilities, estimation, and patterning—topics that we could not cover in our first math book. *Much More Than Counting* is our answer to those suggestions and requests.

Opportunities to solve real-life math problems surround children throughout the classroom, particularly if teachers are aware of the potential and can facilitate the process. Teachers can increase the possibilities for children to engage in mathematical thinking by imbedding opportunities for mathematical reasoning in their plans for each area of the classroom. This increases the opportunities for children to stretch their mathematical thinking throughout the day. Chapter 1 contains ideas for specific activities to increase the math potential in the dramatic play, block, manipulative, sensory, art, music, gross-motor, and outside areas. Suggestions are also included for snack time.

Once young children begin to construct the concept of patterns, they discover that their world is filled with them. Working with patterns provides children with an important foundation for the mathematics they will explore in the years ahead and helps them learn to view items in relationship to one another rather than individually. Chapter 2 includes opportunities for children to explore patterns with many unique materials, from inserting flowers into a sunbonnet to playing musical patterns on cans in the music area.

Estimation is an important component of mathematical reasoning. The ability to estimate helps children evaluate the accuracy of their answers to mathematical problems. Chapter 3 details ways to encourage young children to participate in this process through the use of concrete, intriguing materials. How many of their feet will fit into a T-rex footprint? How many rings stack onto the fingers of a glove? How many little cookies and how many big cookies does it take to fill the cookie jar? These are just a few of the activities that motivate young children to estimate.

Toddlers are dependent upon teachers and caregivers to create a math-rich environment and supply them with the necessary language to further their development. Careful planning of curriculum materials increases the opportunities for the construction of

Chapter 8   Math for Inclusive Classrooms . . 267

Appendix

Chapter 3   Estimation 91

Chapter 4   Math for Toddlers 119

Contents

Acknowledgments

We would like to thank the Arlitt Child and Family Research and Education Center at the University of Cincinnati for its continued support. Facilities, equipment, materials, and children from the center were used in many of the photographs. Staff members graciously cooperated as we rearranged schedules to complete work on this book.

For their willingness to review the manuscript, we thank Anne G. Dorsey, Professor of Early Childhood Education at the University of Cincinnati; Victoria Carr, Associate Director of the Arlitt Center; and Nancy Struewing, Early Childhood Special Education Specialist. Their insights and suggestions were very helpful.

Special thanks go to University of Cincinnati photographer David C. Baxter, for whom *Much More* meant *many more*—more children, more photographs, and more body contortions as he twisted and turned to get just the right angle for each picture.

We appreciate the opportunity to share ideas with other teachers. Several individuals contributed specific activities that we have incorporated into this book: Michael Benton, Nora Cordrey, René Freppon, Lisa Heintz, Dena Papin, Nancy Struewing, and Bob Welker.

We thank Bob Dunnington for his ideas about estimation and Peter Moomaw for his insights into patterning and symmetry and his childhood recollections of the constructions of these concepts. We are indebted to Charles Moomaw for his computer technical support throughout the preparation of the manuscript.

We would like to express our heartfelt appreciation to the staff at Redleaf Press who have worked so hard to make the *More Than* series a reality and have given us a forum for sharing our curriculum ideas with the early childhood field.

Finally, we thank the children who participated in the photos in this book: Ciara, Daniel, Karen, Abby, Andrew, Baxter, Becca, Benjamin, Conner, Daniel, Dominique, Eden, Elias, Evan, Fumi, Haoming, Isaac, Justine, Lilly, Maria, Megan, Molly, Nikhil, Quentin, Safira, Sharon, Sijia, Simone, Sjaya, TiChina, and Wesley.

To the children, families, and staff of the
Arlitt Child and Family Research and Education Center,
University of Cincinnati

How can teachers encourage children who seem to avoid math materials?

Teachers can help children who avoid math materials gain competence and self-confidence in math by subtly including math opportunities in areas of the classroom where the children feel comfortable. Once children feel successful in utilizing math skills, they may eagerly begin using math materials throughout the classroom.

Teachers may find that a slight redesign of an area, so that math becomes a natural part of the play, is enough to encourage reluctant children to begin to explore mathematical concepts. In other instances, the teacher may decide to model the use of math in a play situation. For example, if the teacher has introduced frogs and lily pads into the sensory table as a way of encouraging a child to put objects into a one-to-one correspondence, the teacher might join the play and say, "I wonder if I can find a lily pad for each one of my frogs." The children may quickly incorporate this idea into their play. If the teacher does decide to enter into a play situation, it should be with the intent of modeling a particular type of play rather than directly questioning the children. Such interrogating, however subtle it may seem to the teacher, may discourage rather than encourage children to engage in mathematical play.

How can teachers design the classroom environment to encourage children to think mathematically?

Teachers can introduce new materials into various areas of the classroom or subtly alter materials that are already there. For example, a teacher might include small, plastic teddy bears in the block area during a teddy bear unit. In order to increase the math possibilities, he might later add a small bed and an interactive chart of the song "Ten in the Bed." This encourages children to quantify the bears as they sing each verse of the song. The activities included in this chapter provide suggestions for ways to alter classroom areas to increase their math potential. Teachers can adapt these ideas to fit the interests of the children in their classrooms. However, before teachers redesign areas of their classrooms, they must first decide what mathematical concepts they hope to encourage children to explore.

What math concepts emerge during the preschool and kindergarten years?

Preschool and kindergarten children construct concepts of quantification, one-to-one correspondence, classification, and patterning. They also begin to use the arithmetic operations of addition, subtrac-

tion, multiplication, and division as they attempt to solve real-life problems that emerge during their play or daily classroom life.

Children explore **quantification** and compare sets as they try to figure out how many items they have, or whether or not one person has as much as another. They experiment with the concept of **one-to-one correspondence** throughout their day as they attempt to find one toy for each person, one mitten for each hand, one counter for each space on a game board, or one counting word for each object they are counting. Children think about **classification** as they sort materials by various attributes, such as color, size, or type. They try to put objects, people, or events into meaningful relationships. Once children begin to perceive **patterns,** they may attempt to re-create them, extend them, or create their own.

Although children do not utilize the arithmetic operations in the traditional sense of solving equations, they do construct the underlying concepts as they solve real-life math problems that occur throughout their day. For example, children begin to **add** as they merge groups of toys or materials and count to find the total. They may know what *one more* or *two more* is without having to count. Children **subtract** when they give some of their materials to another child and attempt to find out how much they have left. They think about how many children are left in the room when several are absent or how many ducks are left in a favorite song when one swims away. Children construct the underlying principle of **multiplication** when they have to give several people the same amount of something. For example, if three children each need two rhythm sticks, how many rhythm sticks does the group need? Finally, children are repeatedly confronted with the concept of **division** as they attempt to equitably share materials. Successful teachers encourage children to find their own strategies for solving these problems.

When teachers design areas of the classroom, what are some common pitfalls that affect math potential?

Some teachers have a tendency to put everything out at once. This often overwhelms the children and leads to a very active but less thoughtful type of play. For example, when adding a zoo to the block area, the teacher might put out many types of animals, people, cars, and a train. Having so many materials to deal with at once may overstimulate the children. They may begin dumping the materials rather than using them as block accessories or putting them into logical-mathematical relationships. A better idea might be to start with just a few types of animals, which children can arrange in families, quantify, and incorporate into their block structures. Children might build various sizes of enclosures or see how many animals will fit on each size of block. Later, additional accessories can be introduced.

Teachers often do not put out enough duplicates of materials. Having duplicates encourages children to look for objects that are the same or different (a logical-mathematical relationship) and to quantify to two. Suggestions for the amounts and types of materials to use in various area designs are included in the activities in this chapter.

How can teachers assess children's math levels in play situations?

Teachers can carefully observe children's mathematical problem solving throughout the classroom and record the results anecdotally in each child's file. Some teachers like to record anecdotal notes on file cards and keep them in a file box with a section for each child. Other teachers prefer to divide a notebook into sections, with a pocket divider for each child. Examples of the child's work, such as a score sheet written by the child to record the results of a gross-motor game, can be kept in the pockets for an ongoing portfolio assessment. A running record of the child's classroom experiences can be written on notebook paper and inserted behind the divider. Some teachers keep file folders for each child. Teachers should experiment with various assessment methods to determine the one that best meets their needs. Evaluation of these ongoing anecdotal notes and examples of children's work can guide teachers in their future plans for various areas of the classroom.

What quantification stages will teachers observe in children?

*Teachers will observe children progressing through three stages of quantification: **global, one-to-one correspondence,** and **counting.**[2]* As adults, we often think of counting as the only way to quantify, but children begin to solve mathematical problems long before they are able to understand and employ counting as their strategy for quantifying. Although the age at which children enter the three quantification stages will vary, as will the length of time individual children spend in each stage, the order of the stages is progressive and reflects shifts in children's logical thinking as they develop.

Global—Young children are initially guided by their perceptions when quantifying, and this is reflected in the global stage of quantification. At this level, children make a visual approximation of the quantity they are attempting to match. Thus, if a child wants to take as many crackers as another child, and it looks like that child has a lot of crackers, the child may take a handful as her method of producing an equivalent amount. If asked to take as many teddy bear counters as appear in a sample row, the child may make a row of teddy bears that is approximately the same length as the original row, but disregard the actual number of bears in each row.

One-to-One Correspondence—At this stage, children continue to use their visual or tactile perceptions as a guide for quantifying, but in a much more logical manner. When attempting to take an equivalent amount of a given set, children in the one-to-one correspondence stage will align or match one new item for each object in the original set.

Counting—Children choose counting as their strategy for quantifying or creating an equivalent set when they understand that the last item they count represents the total (**cardinality**). In order to successfully use counting to quantify, children must also realize that there is a particular order to saying the counting words (**stable order**), and each object can be counted only one time, with one number word said for each object counted.[3] This is an application of the concept of **one-to-one correspondence** to counting. At this stage, children count the number of objects in the original set and then count an equivalent number of pieces for their new set. While children may make errors in their counting, the fact that they select counting as their strategy for solving quantification problems shows that they have advanced in their mathematical thinking.

How does assessment guide planning?

Teachers who carefully record ongoing observations of children can use these informal assessments to guide their planning for the class as well as for individual children. For example, if a teacher has a group of children who are largely at the global stage of quantification, she may include more opportunities throughout the classroom for children to explore one-to-one correspondence. This may encourage children to move forward in their thinking to a new level, perhaps at a faster pace than if they had fewer opportunities to think about one-to-one relationships. Likewise, the teacher might create additional opportunities in the classroom to model counting as a quantification strategy if she feels children are ready for more of this type of experience.

Can teachers directly teach mathematical concepts?

No. Mathematical concepts are logical relationships that children must construct for themselves. (The only exception is the name and order of the counting words, which children memorize.) This is why telling children to count objects will not help them to quantify if they have not yet reached the counting stage of quantification. However, the more opportunities children have to confront mathematical problems, the more readily they form mathematical relationships. This is why it is so important for teachers to include opportunities for children to think mathematically throughout the classroom.

What can teachers do to help children construct mathematical concepts?

Teachers can model alternative methods of mathematical problem solving without judging or correcting children on the strategy they are using. It is important for teachers to continually assess children's levels of mathematical thinking so that when teachers choose to enter into play situations, they can model mathematical thinking at or slightly above the level of the children. For example, the teacher might model cardinality for children who do not yet realize that the last number counted represents the total. Thus, while playing in the block area, the teacher might say, "I wonder how many chairs I need for my people. Let's see—one, two, three, four—I have four people, so I need four chairs. Can you help me find four chairs?" If the teacher models mathematical thinking that is too far above the level of the children, they will not be able to reflect on the experience in a meaningful way. This is why the teacher's understanding of children's stages of mathematical thinking is so important.

Teachers can also use leading questions to encourage children to think mathematically. When children encounter a mathematical problem, the teacher can serve as a facilitator. Careful choice of questions can move children forward in their thinking. The following are examples of leading questions that encourage children to think harder or change the direction of their thinking.

▲ How can we tell which row has more?

▲ Is there another way to find out if you both have the same amount?

▲ If two more friends come to our party, will we have enough cups?

▲ How many ice balls do you think will fit in this cup?

What should teachers avoid?

Teachers should avoid solving mathematical problems for children or correcting their errors. Both of these methods discourage children from thinking on their own. We want children to feel confident about their own abilities to think and solve problems. When teachers tell children what methods to use to solve problems, they unintentionally teach children to rely on adults rather than encouraging them to develop their own thinking skills. Whenever people, adults or children alike, attempt to solve new problems, errors inevitably result. It is through these errors that new ways of thinking emerge. Teachers must remind themselves that children's errors are reflections of their current levels of thinking. The mistakes that children make are not permanent and will be resolved as new ways of thinking develop. The more children have to think, the better thinkers they become.

ENDNOTES

1. National Council of Teachers of Mathematics, *Curriculum and Evaluation Standards for School Mathematics* (Reston, VA: NCTM, 1989) 5.
2. Constance Kamii, *Number in Preschool and Kindergarten* (Washington, DC: NAEYC, 1982) 35.
3. Rochel Gelman and C. R. Gallistel, *The Child's Understanding of Number*, 2nd ed. (Cambridge, MA: Harvard UP, 1986) 79.

Math Activities Throughout the Classroom

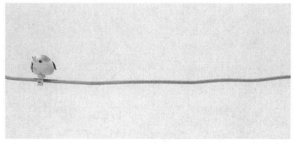

1.1 Cookie Sheets and Cookie Magnets
Dramatic Play Area

Thanks to Bob Welker for this idea.

Description
Many teachers include a bakery in the dramatic play area. For this activity, colored tape is used to divide cookie sheets into boxes, and magnetic cookies fit into the gridded spaces. Children are encouraged to put objects into a one-to-one correspondence relationship as they seek one cookie for each box on the cookie sheet.

Math Concepts
▲ one-to-one correspondence
▲ quantification
▲ addition
▲ subtraction

Materials
▲ cookie sheets, divided into boxes (gridded) with colored tape
▲ cookie magnets, made from plastic cookies with magnetic tape on the backs

Child's Level
This activity is designed for children who are working on one-to-one correspondence. However, the materials are self-leveling, so children with more advanced skills may use them as tools for addition or subtraction.

What to Look For

Many children will place one cookie into each box on the cookie sheets in a one-to-one correspondence relationship.

Some children will quantify the cookies.

Some children will compare the quantities of cookies on various cookie sheets.

Children with more advanced skills may add additional cookies to their cookie sheets and re-count to find the total.

Some children will begin to subtract as they think about how many more cookies they need to fill their cookie sheet.

Modification

Add order forms to the area. Children can write down the orders and then "bake" the necessary number of cookies.

Comments and Questions to Extend Thinking

I wonder if I can find a cookie for each box on my cookie sheet.

How many cookies will you have if James gives you two more?

How many cookies should I bake to fill this order?

How many more cookies do you need to fill all the boxes on your cookie sheet?

How many cookies can each person at the party have?

Integrated Curriculum Activities

Include books about baking in the reading area. *The Doorbell Rang*, by Pat Hutchins (New York: Greenwillow, 1986) and *Bread, Bread, Bread*, by Ann Morris (New York: Lothrop, 1989) are examples.

Bake cookies, pretzels, or muffins with the children.

Create a manipulative game so that children can re-create dividing the cookies in *The Doorbell Rang* (see *More Than Counting*, activity 2.26).

Arrange for a field trip to a bakery.

Graph children's favorite cookies (see *More Than Counting*, chapter 6, for examples).

Helpful Hints

Select cookie sheets that magnets will adhere to. Aluminum cookie sheets will not attract magnets.

Do not make the boxes too big, or children will put more than one cookie in each box and not focus on one-to-one correspondence.

1.2 Egg Cartons and Eggs
Dramatic Play Area

Description

Plastic eggs and egg cartons are easy to add to the dramatic play area. They have great math potential because children attempt to divide the eggs equitably, find out how many eggs they have, or place one egg in each space in the egg carton. The teacher's role in modeling, commenting, or asking leading questions increases the mathematical value of the experience.

Math Concepts

▲ one-to-one correspondence
▲ quantification
▲ addition
▲ subtraction
▲ multiplication
▲ division

Materials

▲ plastic or Styrofoam egg cartons
▲ plastic or wooden eggs

Child's Level

This activity is popular with a wide range of children, from young preschoolers, who like to put one egg into each space in the egg carton, to older preschool or kindergarten children, who may add, subtract, or divide the eggs.

Helpful Hints

Be sure the egg cartons are thoroughly cleaned and sanitized to avoid any risk of food poisoning.

What to Look For

Many children will fill each space in the egg carton with an egg (one-to-one correspondence).

Children will use a variety of strategies to try to divide the eggs equitably.

Some children will count to see how many eggs they have.

Children will compare how many eggs each person has.

Some children will give the same number of eggs to each person and then quantify the eggs (multiplication).

Children may give away some of their eggs and then determine how many eggs are left (subtraction).

Modification

Add menus and order forms to the area. Children can write down and fill the orders. This encourages them to quantify and compare sets.

Comments and Questions to Extend Thinking

How many more eggs do you need to fill your egg carton?

Do you have enough eggs for each space in the egg carton?

If you give two eggs each to Amanda, Claire, and Jeff, how many eggs will you need?

How can we divide these eggs so we each have the same amount?

If Sanjay gives you one more egg, how many eggs will you have?

How can we find out who has the most eggs?

I would like two eggs, and Matthew wants three. Do you have enough?

Integrated Curriculum Activities

Over a period of several days, cook and prepare eggs in a variety of ways. Boiled eggs, scrambled eggs, and egg salad are possibilities.

Visit a farm to collect eggs, or take a walk to a local store to buy them.

Add bird nests to the science area (see *More Than Magnets*, activity 2.8).

Put a bird nest and egg game in the manipulative or math area (see *More Than Counting*, activity 2.2).

1.3 Hat Shop
Dramatic Play Area

Description
Children love dressing up in hats. This design of the dramatic play area allows children to dramatize the classic children's book *Caps for Sale,* by Esphyr Slobodkina (Reading, MA: Addison-Wesley, 1968). They can quantify hats as they stack them on their heads or hand them to a friend. Children can also apply math skills by paying for the hats with pennies. The price tags should have picture representations of the pennies so that children in all three stages of quantification (global, one-to-one correspondence, or counting) can create equivalent sets.

Math Concepts
▲ quantification
▲ addition
▲ division
▲ one-to-one correspondence

Materials
▲ variety of dress-up hats and caps, preferably multicultural
▲ pennies
▲ price tags made from note cards, with quantities of pennies from 1 to 10 traced and colored in on the cards
▲ cash register (optional)

Child's Level
This activity is most appropriate for older preschool and kindergarten children who will not put the pennies in their mouths.

What to Look For

Children will try to stack hats on their heads like the peddler in *Caps for Sale*.

Children will quantify the number of hats they can balance on their heads.

Children will compare the number of hats they can balance.

Some children may give each child or doll one hat (one-to-one correspondence).

Children may try to divide the hats among all the participants.

Children will select a quantification strategy based on their level of development—global, one-to-one correspondence, or counting.

Some children will place one penny on each picture of a penny on the price tag to find out how many pennies they need.

Modifications

For younger children, eliminate the price tags and pennies. These children may be interested in placing the hats on themselves or the dolls in one-to-one correspondence.

For children who understand cardinality and can recognize numerals, use numerals for the price tags rather than pictures of pennies, and include larger prices.

Questions to Extend Thinking

How many hats can you stack on your head?

How many pennies do I need to pay for this hat?

If I buy these two hats, how many pennies do I need?

How can we divide the hats so that each customer has the same number?

Integrated Curriculum Activities

Include books about hats in the reading area. *Aunt Flossie's Hats*, by Elizabeth Fitzgerald Howard (New York: Clarion, 1991), *Hats, Hats, Hats*, by Ann Morris (New York: Lothrop, 1989), and *Who Took the Farmer's Hat?* by Joan L. Nodset (New York: Harper, 1963) are examples.

Place a collection of small hats in the manipulative area for sorting and classifying (see *More Than Counting*, activity 3.4).

Graph the children's hats.

Helpful Hints

Painters' caps and plastic visors can be obtained inexpensively from party and craft stores.

Ask parents to donate hats and caps.

1.4 Shoe Store
Dramatic Play Area

Description
Children are always interested in their shoes. In this dramatic play arrangement, children can select and purchase shoes and pay for them with pennies. The shoes reflect a variety of cultures.

Math Concepts
▲ quantification
▲ one-to-one correspondence
▲ addition
▲ multiplication

Materials
▲ a variety of shoes, preferably from several cultures
▲ price tags ranging from 1 to 10 cents, made by gluing pennies onto note cards and sealing them in zip lock bags
▲ pennies
▲ cash register (optional)

Child's Level
This area is appropriate for both preschool and kindergarten children. Teachers can adjust the price tags depending on the quantification levels of the children.

What to Look For
Children will quantify the pennies as they attempt to pay for the shoes.

Children will select a quantification strategy based on their level of development—global, one-to-one correspondence, or counting.

Some children will add quantities of pennies when they purchase more than one pair of shoes.

Modifications

For very young children who may still put objects in their mouths, substitute larger counters, such as poker chips, for the pennies. Limit quantities on the price tags to three.

For children who understand cardinality and recognize numerals, teachers can make price tags that use numerals instead of pennies and increase the prices of the shoes so that children can work with larger amounts.

Questions to Extend Thinking

How many pennies do I need to pay for this pair of shoes?

If I buy these two pairs of shoes, how much money do I need?

How can Steve find out if he has enough pennies for the shoes he wants to buy?

If Brady and Ryan each buy three pairs of shoes, how many shoes will that be?

Integrated Curriculum Activities

Dip small shoes from key chains or novelty stores in paint to make imprints.

Graph the children's shoes by a variety of attributes, such as color, type of shoe, or type of shoe fastener (see *More Than Counting*, activity 6.3).

Read books about shoes, such as *Red Dancing Shoes*, by Denise Lewis Patrick (New York: Tambourine, 1993), *Two Pairs of Shoes*, by Esther Sanderson (Winnipeg, Canada: Pemmican, 1990), and *Where Did You Get Your Moccasins?* by Bernalda Wheeler (Winnipeg, Canada: Pequis, 1992).

Place a small tub of sand and a variety of small novelty shoes in the science area. Children can create footprints with them (see *More Than Magnets*, activity 2.14).

Helpful Hints

Check import stores or shops in culturally diverse areas of cities for shoes from various cultures. Parents are also a good source.

Use clear tape to seal the price tags in plastic sandwich bags so that children can see the pennies but cannot remove them.

1.5 Ice-Cream Parlor
Dramatic Play Area

Description
Children love ordering ice-cream treats or filling other children's orders in this design of the dramatic play area. Large pompoms that are the colors of ice cream flavors substitute for scoops of ice cream, and cardboard yarn spools make realistic-looking cones.

The math opportunities abound as children quantify the type and number of scoops ordered and collect payment. Other props include visors, ice-cream spoons, dishes, and menus.

Math Concepts
▲ quantification
▲ one-to-one correspondence
▲ addition
▲ multiplication

Materials
▲ large pompoms (approximately 2 inches in diameter) that are the colors of ice-cream flavors
▲ cardboard spools or plastic funnels, to use as cones
▲ menus (as pictured), with prices ranging from 1 to 10 cents
▲ pennies

Child's Level
This activity is most appropriate for older preschool and kindergarten children, although younger children certainly enjoy participating in the play.

What to Look For
Children will quantify as they fill ice-cream orders, such as two scoops of chocolate and one scoop of vanilla.

Some children will put one pompom on each cone or in each dish in a one-to-one correspondence relationship.

Children will help each other decide how much they have to pay and if they have given the correct number of pennies to the clerk.

Modifications

If the menus and money are overwhelming to the children, add them to the area at a later time after the children are familiar with the materials.

If some of the prices on the menu are too high for children to quantify, change the menus to range from 1 to 5 cents per item.

Comments and Questions to Extend Thinking

I want two scoops of strawberry and two scoops of chocolate, please.

If I order two scoops of ice cream, how much do I have to pay?

Jeff, Amanda, and Rachel each want two scoops. How many is that?

Who can help me read the menu?

Does a soda cost more than a sundae?

Integrated Curriculum Activities

Make ice cream with the children by rolling it in cans (see *More Than Magnets,* activity 7.6).

Clap ice-cream flavors for a rhythm activity (see *More Than Singing,* chapter 3).

Add ice-cream patterning or math manipulative games to the manipulative area (activities 2.1 and 5.8).

Helpful Hints

The menus are made from white construction paper and stickers. Laminate the menus before writing the prices in permanent marker. Then, if you need to change the prices to meet the mathematical levels of your class, you can remove the old prices with alcohol and won't have to make new menus.

1.6 Parking Lot
Block Area

Description
To encourage children to think about one-to-one correspondence, a wooden bench in the block area is turned into a parking lot. Colored tape divides the bench into a grid with parking spaces for toy vehicles.

Math Concepts
▲ one-to-one correspondence
▲ quantification
▲ sorting and classifying
▲ addition
▲ subtraction
▲ division

Materials
▲ wooden bench, wooden plank, or piece of heavy cardboard
▲ colored tape
▲ small toy vehicles
▲ toy parking meters (optional)

Helpful Hints

Be sure the parking spaces are large enough for just one vehicle each if you want children to focus on one-to-one correspondence.

Child's Level
This activity is most appropriate for preschool children. Kindergarten children working on one-to-one correspondence may also benefit from this activity.

What to Look For
Children will put one vehicle into each parking space in a one-to-one correspondence relationship.

Some children will sort the vehicles by a particular attribute, such as color or type, and park similar vehicles together.

Children may count empty spaces to see how many more vehicles they can park.

Children will use various strategies to divide the vehicles among themselves.

Modification
Use fewer parking spaces with younger children. They may become overwhelmed if there are too many spaces. Six to eight spaces is an appropriate number for young children.

Comments and Questions to Extend Thinking
Do you have enough cars to park one in each parking space?

Abby has two cars, and so do I. If I give her my two cars, how many will she have?

How many more vehicles do you need to fill up the parking lot?

How many cars didn't get a parking space?

How can we divide these cars so that everyone has the same number?

Integrated Curriculum Activities
Use small vehicles as painting tools (see *More Than Magnets,* activity 5.10).

Roll toy cars down ramps of varying slopes in the science area (see *More Than Magnets,* activity 3.2).

1.7 Animal Families
Block Area

Description

Many teachers include toy animals as accessories in the block area. This activity shows a particular way to set up such materials to encourage mathematical thinking and problem solving in young children.

Math Concepts

▲ sorting and classifying
▲ quantification
▲ comparison of sets

Materials

▲ 5 plastic animal families, each consisting of 1 adult and 2 babies
▲ 1 additional adult of each type of animal, to add after the first week

Child's Level
This activity is most appropriate for young preschool children.

What to Look For
Children will group the baby animals with the corresponding adult animals.

Children will compare the number of baby animals and adult animals in each family.

Some children will quantify the animals.

Modifications
Add a second adult animal for each family grouping after the first week. This will allow children to form new mathematical relationships with the animals.

For older children, supply varying amounts of babies and alter the questions accordingly.

Questions to Extend Thinking
Which animals go together?

Are there more mommies or babies?

How many babies does the sheep mommy have?

How many more grown-up animals do we need to give each family a daddy?

Integrated Curriculum Activities
Read books about animal families, such as *Time for Bed,* by Mem Fox (New York: Harcourt, 1997).

Let the class make animal footprints. Look for rubber stamps or plastic animals that make animal footprints.

Clap animal words for a rhythmic activity (see *More Than Singing,* chapter 3).

Design animal path games (see activities 7.4b and 8.9).

Helpful Hints

If possible, set the animals on a low bench in the block area. This encourages children to group them and observe the results.

1.8 Hide the Ducks
Block Area

Description
This activity introduces five plastic ducks into the block area.
Children take turns hiding several ducks in a small duck house,
perhaps made with the blocks. The other children look at the
remaining ducks and try to determine how many are hidden. This
game could also be incorporated into the manipulative area or sensory table. It is an extension of the familiar children's song "Five
Little Ducks" (see *More Than Singing,* p. 178).

Math Concepts
▲ subtraction
▲ quantification

Helpful Hints

Substitute other toy ani-
mals, such as bears, for
the ducks if desired.

Materials
▲ 5 small plastic ducks
▲ duck house, made from blocks or a small box

Child's Level
This activity is most appropriate for older preschool or kindergarten children. Younger children may use the ducks in other ways
that are appropriate for their level of thinking, such as reenacting
the song with the ducks.

What to Look For

Children will use a variety of strategies to determine how many ducks are hidden.

Some children will *count on* to find out how many ducks are left. They will start with the number of ducks they can see and count the missing ducks on their fingers until they reach five.

Some children will quantify the ducks they can see but be unable to figure out how many ducks are hidden.

Children will watch one another and discuss ways to solve the missing ducks problem.

Some children will use the ducks to act out the verses of the "Five Little Ducks" song.

Modification

Include additional ducks for children who are adept at subtracting from five.

Comments and Questions to Extend Thinking

I see one, two, three, four ducks outside the duck house. I wonder how many ducks are inside.

If one more duck goes into the duck house, how many ducks will be left outside?

How did you decide how many ducks are hidden?

Integrated Curriculum Activities

Put plastic ducks in the water table.

Use duck cookie cutters with playdough.

Add a book version of the song "Five Little Ducks" to the reading area. Teachers can make their own book with duck stickers.

Make a class duck book. Children can illustrate the pages and dictate or write their own duck stories.

1.9 Frogs on Lily Pads
Sensory Table

Description
In this activity, small plastic frogs and pretend lily pads provide the incentive for children to think about one-to-one correspondence and quantification. The teacher's questions can further direct children's thinking along these lines.

Math Concepts
▲ one-to-one correspondence
▲ quantification
▲ addition
▲ subtraction
▲ multiplication
▲ division

Materials
▲ approximately 12 small plastic frogs
▲ green plastic coasters or lids (approximately 3 inches in diameter), to use as lily pads (1 per frog)
▲ sensory table with water
▲ fishing nets (optional)

Child's Level
This activity is appropriate for many children. Younger children may focus on one-to-one correspondence and put one frog on each lily pad. Older children may use the frogs for addition, subtraction, or multiplication.

What to Look For
Many children will put one frog on each lily pad in a one-to-one correspondence relationship.

Some children will add additional frogs to the lily pads.

Children may put the same number of frogs on several lily pads and quantify the results (multiplication).

Children may devise strategies to divide the frogs equitably.

Some sets of plastic frogs vary by color, size, and design. Children may sort these frogs by their various attributes.

Modifications

For children on the one-to-one correspondence level, make the lily pads close to the same size as the frogs. This will encourage them to put just one frog on each lily pad.

For older or more advanced children, use larger lily pads and more frogs. This will encourage addition and multiplication as children put varying quantities of frogs on the lily pads.

Comments and Questions to Extend Thinking

Do you have enough frogs to put one on each lily pad?

If I put one more frog on this lily pad, I wonder how many I'll have.

How many more frogs are sitting on this lily pad than on this one?

Look! Tuukka has three lily pads, and they each have two frogs. How many frogs is that?

How many frogs will you have left if one hops into the water?

Integrated Curriculum Activities

Read books about frogs, such as *Jump, Frog, Jump,* by Robert Kalan (New York: Greenwillow, 1981).

Watch a tadpole transform into a frog. Children can chart the changes.

Set up a "frog hopping" game in the gross-motor area. Children roll a giant die and hop along large lily pads cut from heavy paper or cardboard (see *More Than Counting,* chapter 7, for examples of gross-motor path games).

1.10 Ice Cube Trays and Balls
Sensory Table

Description
Children love fishing for ice balls with tongs or nets. The ice cube trays encourage children to think about one-to-one correspondence as they attempt to put one ice ball in each compartment. Children also like to quantify the ice balls.

Math Concepts
▲ one-to-one correspondence
▲ quantification
▲ addition

Materials
▲ ice balls
▲ ice cube trays
▲ sensory table with water
▲ tongs or fishing nets (optional)

Child's Level
This activity is most appropriate for preschool children.

What to Look For
Children will put one ice ball in each compartment of the ice cube trays in a one-to-one correspondence relationship.
Some children will quantify the ice balls.
Children may sort the ice balls by color.

Modification
For older children who are working with larger quantities, substitute ice cube trays that hold many small cubes. Use marbles instead of ice balls to fit the smaller holes in the ice trays.

Comments and Questions to Extend Thinking
Can you catch enough ice balls to put one in each hole of your tray?
How many more ice balls do you need to fill up your tray?
I wonder how many balls this tray will hold.
If you catch two balls in your net, will you have enough to fill your tray?

Integrated Curriculum Activities
After the children have had experience with ice balls, add large marbles to the water table. Children can compare the buoyancy of the marbles with the ice balls.
Let children freeze some of the ice balls and compare them to unfrozen ice balls.

Check dollar stores or odd-lot stores for a wide variety of inexpensive ice cube trays and ice balls.

1.11 Gridded Easel Paper
Art Area

Description
For this activity, lines are drawn on easel paper to divide the paper into large boxes. Many children respond to this type of paper by putting one mark, shape, or painted object into each box. This encourages them to think about one-to-one correspondence. Other children may create patterns or draw objects in sequence.

Math Concepts
▲ one-to-one correspondence
▲ patterning
▲ sequencing

Materials
▲ easel, with paint or markers
▲ easel paper, with lines drawn to create a grid

Child's Level
Children respond to gridded easel paper in different ways, depending on their ages and levels of thinking. Therefore, this activity is appropriate for both preschool and kindergarten children.

Helpful Hints
Gridded paper can be used on a flat surface, such as a table, if an easel is not available.

What to Look For

Children will paint one mark, shape, or picture in each box in a
one-to-one correspondence relationship.

Some children will use the boxes to create patterns, such as
alternating colors or shapes.

Older children may view the boxes as a structure for sequencing.
They may arrange a story or draw quantities of items in
sequential order.

Modification

To encourage patterning, start with two colors of paint. Children
often decide to alternate the colors in the boxes.

Comments and Questions to Extend Thinking

What will you do with all the boxes on the paper?
I notice that you have one picture in each box.
How did you decide which color to put in each box?

Integrated Curriculum Activities

Include grid games in the math or manipulative areas (see
chapter 6 for examples).

Introduce a variety of painting tools to use with the gridded paper
(see *More Than Painting*, chapter 5, for examples).

1.12 Press-On Dots and Graph Paper

Art Area

Description

This activity combines round stickers with 1-inch graph paper. It encourages young children to think about one-to-one correspondence and older children to create patterns.

Math Concepts

▲ one-to-one correspondence
▲ patterning

Materials

▲ ¾-inch round stickers, in assorted colors
▲ 1-inch graph paper

Child's Level

This activity is most appropriate for older preschool or kindergarten children. Younger children may have trouble coordinating the stickers with the graph paper.

What to Look For

Some children will place one sticker in each box on the graph paper in a one-to-one correspondence relationship.

Some children will sort the stickers by color. They may create rows of each color.

Some children will create patterns or designs with the stickers.

Some children will use the stickers to create representational pictures within the confines of the graph paper.

Modification

Try using ¼-inch graph paper and ¼-inch file folder stickers for older children.

Comments and Questions to Extend Thinking

Nancy created a pattern. Can you tell which color she'll put next?

Is there another pattern you can create with these colors?

If you put one sticker in each box, how many stickers do you need for each row?

Integrated Curriculum Activities

Substitute bingo paint markers for stickers to vary the activity.

Read the book *Little Blue and Little Yellow,* by Leo Lionni (New York: Astor-Honor, 1959). The characters are blobs of color similar to the stickers.

Use plastic bingo markers for cover-ups on a grid game (see chapter 6 for examples).

Helpful Hints

To encourage patterning, try starting with just two colors of stickers. Many children will use two colors to create alternating patterns, but they may be overwhelmed at first by too many colors.

1.13 Flowerpot Sound Patterns
Music Area

Description
A music area in the classroom allows children to explore instruments and create sounds. The way the area is set up may also encourage children to create patterns of sound. This activity shows teachers how to introduce patterning and counting into the music area with suspended flowerpots. Each size pot resonates with its own relative pitch.

Math Concepts
▲ patterning
▲ quantification

Materials
▲ 3 sizes of flowerpots, suspended with fishing line from a wooden frame or pegboard divider
▲ wooden mallets or sticks, for striking the flowerpots

Child's Level
This activity is appropriate for both preschool and kindergarten children.

What to Look For
Children will start by experimenting with the pots. They may hit them with the mallets and compare the sounds they make.
Some children will repeatedly play the pots in order, thus creating a pattern.
Children may listen to what the teacher or other children play and attempt to reproduce it.
Children may create a variety of sound patterns on the pots.

Modifications
To encourage patterning with younger children, start with two pots. This suggests an alternating pattern to many children.
Add additional sizes of flowerpots for older or more experienced children. Teachers can also tape-record sound patterns played on the pots for children to try to duplicate.

Comments and Questions to Extend Thinking

Can you play your flowerpot the same number of times that I play mine?

Listen to Samudra's pattern. What should come next?

Can you use these pots to create a pattern?

I'm going to start a pattern. See if you can keep playing it after I stop.

Can we combine some patterns to make a song?

See if you can play the same thing Kisha plays.

Integrated Curriculum Activities

Play sound patterns on the flowerpots at group time. Children can try to guess the patterns. This may encourage children to create their own patterns in the music area.

Paint flowerpots with acrylic paint and then plant seeds or house-plants in them.

Read books that describe creating music on found objects. *Max Found Two Sticks,* by Brian Pinkney (New York: Simon, 1994) and *Max the Music Maker,* by Miriam B. Stechler and Alice S. Kandell (New York: Lothrop, 1980) are examples.

Include books about planting, such as *Flower Garden,* by Eve Bunting (New York: Harcourt, 1994) in the reading area.

Introduce other instruments in the music area for children to use to create patterns (see *More Than Singing,* chapter 5, and *More Than Magnets,* chapter 6, for examples).

1.14 One, Two, Three—Jump!
Gross-Motor Area

Description
Children love to have the teacher or a friend count before they jump. This activity shows teachers how to introduce counting into a typical large muscle activity.

Math Concept
stable order counting

Materials
▲ climber, box, or platform for children to jump off
▲ mat or padding for safety

Child's Level
This activity is most appropriate for preschool children who are working on stable order counting. It can also be used with kindergarten children who are not yet secure with counting.

Helpful Hints
Children also like to count in other languages once they are secure with counting in English.

What to Look For
Children will eagerly wait for the designated number
  before they jump.
Children will select numbers for the teacher to count to
  before they jump.
Children will count along with the teacher as they learn
  the order of the counting words.
Children may count for each other before they jump.

Modifications
Start with small numbers for children who are just beginning to
  count—perhaps up to three. Increase the number as children
  become ready.
Teachers can model counting backwards or counting by 2s or 5s
  for older children who may be working on these concepts.

Questions to Extend Thinking
How high should I count before you jump?
Who wants to help me count for Hinoko?

Integrated Curriculum Activities
Sing counting songs at group time. "Three Little Bats" and "Salty
  Pretzels" (*More Than Counting,* activities 2.14 and 2.25) and
  "Five Little Ducks" (*More Than Singing,* activity 6.9) are popular
  examples.
Count while children perform a variety of movements—nodding,
  jumping, stretching, stamping, clapping, etc.

1.15 Hop to the Mitten
Gross-Motor Area

Description

Many children are attracted to *The Mitten,* a Ukrainian story in which a series of animals manage to fit inside a lost mitten. Several book versions are available. In this gross-motor math game, children roll a giant die and hop along a path made from carpet squares. They each carry a laminated drawing of one of the animals from the story to hang on a large paper mitten at the end of the path.

Math Concepts
▲ quantification
▲ one-to-one correspondence
▲ creation and comparison of sets

Materials
▲ 10 to 12 carpet squares, to form the path
▲ 1–6 die, made from a large stuffed fabric cube with 1 to 6 dots on each side
▲ large mitten, cut from paper and mounted to the wall
▲ drawings of the characters from the story
▲ magnetic tape, cut into small pieces and mounted on the mitten and on the back of the drawings

Child's Level
This activity is most appropriate for older preschool or kindergarten children.

Helpful Hints

Laminate the animal drawings before attaching the magnetic tape. The mitten shape may be too large to laminate.

Use puffy paint to paint the dots on the die.

What to Look For

Many children will roll the die and hop an equivalent number
of spaces along the path. They will carry an animal to attach
to the mitten.

When playing table-sized path games, many children recount the
square their mover already occupies each time they take a turn.
They often do not make this error when *they* are the movers.

A few children may be more successful playing this gross-motor
path game than playing path games in the classroom.

Some children may hop to the end of the path without regard to
the quantity on the die.

Some children will count the number of animals in the mitten.

Modification

For younger or less experienced children, reduce the number of
dots on the die to three.

Comments and Questions to Extend Thinking

How many spaces will you hop along the path?

Stacy hopped one space for this dot and one space for this dot.
(Point to each dot as you make this comment.)

How many more spaces until you can put the fox in the mitten?

How many animals are in the mitten so far?

If Antonio puts the rabbit in the mitten, how many animals will
there be?

Integrated Curriculum Activities

Include a book version of this Ukrainian story in the classroom.
One popular example is *The Mitten,* by Jan Brett (New York:
Putnam, 1989).

Assemble a collection of toy animals from the story and a mitten
to place them in. Children can reenact the story as they look at
the book.

Put toddler mittens in the dramatic play area for children to use
with dolls.

Sing songs about snow (see *More Than Singing,* activities 2.6, 4.5,
and 6.6).

Put collage materials that resemble snow in the art area. Cotton
balls, pieces of white tissue paper, white and silver glitter, and
white confetti are possibilities (see *More Than Painting,*
activity 2.7).

1.16 Baby Stroller Game
Outside Area

Description
For this game, lines are painted across a sidewalk to create a path, such as on a board game. Children with doll strollers are the movers. The children roll a giant die to determine how many spaces to push their stroller along the path. When they reach the end, they can select a toy for their doll baby.

Math Concepts
▲ quantification
▲ one-to-one correspondence
▲ addition

Materials
▲ a 1–6 die, made from a large stuffed fabric cube with 1 to 6 dots on each side
▲ tempera paint, used to paint lines on the sidewalk
▲ doll strollers and dolls
▲ baby toys

Child's Level
This activity is appropriate for either preschool or kindergarten children.

What to Look For

Children will roll the die to determine how many spaces to push their strollers.

Children will use various strategies (global, one-to-one correspondence, or counting) to decide how many spaces to move.

Children who are not yet ready to quantify may push their strollers along the path without regard to how many dots they rolled on the die.

Children may correct one another when they feel a mistake has been made.

Some children will play the game repeatedly to collect more toys for their dolls.

Modifications

Use a 1–3 die for children who are just beginning to quantify while playing path games.

Use two dice for children who are ready to add two sets together.

Questions to Extend Thinking

How can you tell how many spaces to push your stroller?

If you get two on your next roll, will you reach the end?

How many more do you need to reach the end?

Integrated Curriculum Activities

Add math games about babies to the manipulative or math area (activities 6.9, 7.9a, and 7.9b).

Sing "Hush, Little Baby" with the children's names (see *More Than Singing,* activity 2.13).

Change the dramatic play area into a baby nursery.

Wash dolls in the sensory table.

Include books about babies, such as *Hush!* by Minfong Ho (New York: Orchard, 1996) and *More, More, More Said the Baby,* by Vera B. Williams (New York: Greenwillow, 1990), in the reading area.

Helpful Hints

Chalk can be substituted for paint to create the path. Both will eventually wash away, but paint lasts longer than chalk.

Look for large dice in the automotive area of stores.

Dice can be made by sticking round dots on Styrofoam cubes or by painting dots on sewn cubes that have been stuffed.

1.17 Gridded Napkins
Snack

Description
This activity encourages children to place finger foods, such as grapes or celery sticks, in a one-to-one correspondence relationship with the grid spaces on their napkins. Children may also wish to count their snack items. Teachers can use colored pencils or pens to draw grid lines on the napkins. The idea for this activity came from observations of children, who often put one cracker or cookie into each space created by the folds of their napkins.

Math Concepts
▲ one-to-one correspondence
▲ quantification
▲ addition
▲ subtraction
▲ multiplication

Materials
▲ paper napkins, with lines drawn on them to form grids
▲ finger food snacks

Child's Level
This activity is appropriate for both preschool and kindergarten, since children of different ages respond very differently to the materials. Younger children typically focus on one-to-one correspondence, while older children may use the items for arithmetic operations.

What to Look For

Children may put one snack item in each grid space in a one-to-one correspondence relationship.

Children may count to find out how many pieces of food they have.

Children may compare quantities of food with one another.

Some children may take additional pieces of a snack food and add them to their previous amount to get the total.

Some children may subtract as they eat some of the food and attempt to find out how much is left.

Some children may put the same number of food items in each grid space and quantify the results (multiplication).

Modification

For younger children, draw fewer boxes on the napkins so that they are not overwhelmed by the number of spaces.

Questions to Extend Thinking

Do you have enough crackers to put one in each box?

How many grapes will you have if you fill every box?

If you eat two carrot sticks, how many will you have left?

How many more celery sticks do you need to fill all of your boxes?

If you put two goldfish crackers in each box, how many goldfish will you have?

If you take two more apple pieces, how many will you have?

Integrated Curriculum Activities

Use gridded paper for art activities (see activities 1.11 and 1.12).

Add gridded place mats to the dramatic play area.

Make a food grid game for the manipulative or math area. Small wooden vegetables make interesting counters (see *More Than Counting*, activity 4.4).

Do not use watercolor markers to draw the grid lines on the napkins. Watercolor markers will smear if they become wet and the ink may get on the food.

1.18 Goldfish Cracker Story
Snack

Description
The following story, or a similar one created by the teacher or a child, can encourage children to think mathematically as they reenact the story with their snack crackers.

▲ ▲ ▲

Once four goldfish were swimming in a pond. A little girl and her friend were fishing in the pond, and they each caught a goldfish.
How many were left?
The girls felt sorry for the fish,
so they threw them back into
the pond. Soon another fish joined the group.
How many fish were there now?
A hungry turtle ate one of the fish.
How many were left?
Then a man caught two of the fish in a net and put them in a bowl to take home.
How many fish were left?
What do you think happened next?

Math Concepts
▲ quantification
▲ addition
▲ subtraction

Materials
▲ goldfish crackers
▲ napkins (preferably blue)

Child's Level
Both preschool and kindergarten children find this activity challenging and interesting.

What to Look For
Children will use the goldfish crackers to act out the story.
Children will add and subtract as they requantify the fish.
Some children will extend the story or make up their own stories.
Some children will eat all of their crackers as they listen to the story!

Modifications
Start with fewer crackers for younger children. Simplify both the story and the math by only adding or subtracting by one.
Use more goldfish with children who are more experienced with addition and subtraction. Teachers can create stories that emphasize particular number combinations that children may be working on.

Questions to Extend Thinking
The questions for this activity are imbedded in the story.

Integrated Curriculum Activities
Put plastic fish and fishing nets in the water table.
Read books about fish, such as *Swimmy,* by Leo Lionni (New York: Knopf, 1963), and *Blue Sea,* by Robert Kalan (New York: Green-willow, 1979).
Sing songs about fish, such as "Swish, Swish, Swish" (see *More Than Singing,* activity 2.15).
Make water maracas with the children by partially filling clear plastic bottles with colored water and sealing the lids.
Compile children's fish stories into a class book.
Let children dramatize some of the fish stories at group time.

Helpful Hints

Try similar stories for animal crackers, teddy-shaped grahams, and even cereal O's.

Patterns and Symmetry

At going home time, Molly approached her teacher excitedly to show him a repeating pattern she had made with 1-inch colored cubes. Just then, the school receptionist announced over the intercom that Molly's carpool was waiting for her. Molly was very disappointed. Now she couldn't show her pattern to her friends. "Don't worry, Molly," said Ismail. "I can copy your pattern on this paper." Ismail brought a piece of graph paper from the art area and began to color in the boxes to match Molly's pattern. When Molly arrived at school the next day, a copy of her pattern was waiting for her in her cubby. She happily showed it to all of her friends.

▲ ▲ ▲

Once young children become aware of patterns, they begin to explore them throughout their world. They may create patterns, as Molly did, or reproduce patterns, as her friend Ismail did. Working with patterns provides children with an important foundation for the mathematics they will explore in the years ahead.

Teachers' Questions
What is a pattern?

A pattern involves a repeating element. Items in a pattern might appear in a sequence that repeats, such as colored beads strung in a repeating order of red–blue–green, red–blue–green. A pattern can also involve an underlying repeating quality, such as a mathematical operation that is performed on each number in a sequence. For example, the numbers *2, 4, 6, 8* exhibit a pattern in which each number is two more than the previous number in the sequence. Although the numbers themselves do not repeat, the pattern of adding two to each number does.

Why is patterning an important mathematical concept?

Perceiving patterns helps children understand mathematical structures. Mathematical thinking involves constructing relationships among ideas and concepts. Although not all mathematical relationships involve patterns, exploring patterns helps children learn to view items in relationship to one another rather than individually. Formation of these logical-mathematical relationships is the basis of future mathematical problem solving.

Unfortunately, teachers have a tendency to teach mathematical concepts, including patterning, by rote rather than by facilitating children's construction of the underlying relationships. For example, teachers often require children to memorize the even numbers in order. However, this is essentially useless information until children construct the underlying relationship that each number is two more than the previous number. A child who perceives this pattern can quickly give the next even number after a large number, such as 642; a child who does not recognize the relationship among the even numbers may not be able to solve the problem.

Are young children interested in patterns?

Young children become very interested in patterns once they begin to perceive them. This may occur for some children after the teacher has helped them discover patterns around the classroom. Children often become particularly interested in patterns on their own clothing. As with all mathematical relationships, children vary in how quickly they construct concepts of patterning. In general, older preschool and kindergarten children seem to more quickly understand the concept of a pattern than younger children.

What concepts do young children construct related to patterns?

Children learn to recognize, extend, and create patterns once they understand the underlying relationship among the items forming the patterns. While patterning relationships cannot be directly taught to children, teachers can facilitate the construction of patterning concepts by planning activities that expose children to patterns and providing them with materials for creating their own. For example, children may learn to recognize patterns in teacher-designed pattern strips, particularly if the patterns are introduced at group time and chanted rhythmically. Children can place manipulative pieces in the empty boxes on the strips to extend the patterns (see activities 2.3, 2.4, and 2.12). Children begin to create patterns once they become aware of the patterns around them. They often create patterns in their art work, such as stringing beads or painting stripes in a repeating color order.

Children may also construct some mathematical relationships built on patterns. The realization that, when counting, each number is one more than the previous number, or the discovery that even and odd numbers alternate are examples of mathematical relationships that involve patterns.

What are the easiest patterns for young children to recognize?

The simplest patterns are alternating patterns in which the items vary by only one attribute, such as color. Alternating red and blue pegs is an example; stringing spherical and cubical beads is another. It is important to vary only one attribute, since young children have trouble focusing on more than one aspect of the pattern at a time. Therefore, to help children perceive a pattern that involves different bead shapes, keep the colors the same.

What are more complex patterns?

Patterns that are longer, have some items that repeat within the pattern, or involve more than one attribute are more complicated for children to recognize. Teachers can increase the length of a pattern by adding additional items, such as sequences of three or more colors (green–white–black; green–white–black). Repeating an item within a pattern adds more complexity (green–white–white–black; green–white–white–black). Finally, varying two or more attributes makes patterns much more complicated for young children to perceive (green triangle–white circle–white triangle; green triangle–white circle–white triangle).

What areas of the classroom provide opportunities for patterning?

The art, block, manipulative, science, and music areas are all good settings for teachers to introduce patterning activities. Planning patterning activities for many classroom areas allows children to use a variety of types of materials to form patterning relationships. It also encourages children who are more comfortable in some areas of the classroom than in others to explore patterning. The activities included in this chapter introduce patterning into all of the areas listed above.

How can teachers utilize classroom environments to encourage children to create patterns?

Teachers can help children discover patterns that exist naturally throughout their environment, both indoors and outdoors. From alternating colors of floor tiles to the stripes on their own clothes, children are surrounded by patterns. It is the teacher's role to draw attention to patterns and initiate discussions about them so that children begin to discover patterns themselves.

Teachers can also design specific materials and activities that encourage children to create and extend patterns. As children interact with the materials and with one another, their ability to use the same objects to create many different relationships increases. This helps young children develop more flexible thinking and problem-solving capabilities.

Teachers may occasionally model creating patterns to help get children started. They may ask leading questions to draw children's attention toward patterns. When teachers model, it should be with the intent of showing another way to use the materials, not the "correct" way. If children show an interest in patterns, they can continue on their own. If they are not interested in creating patterns, the teacher can wait for another opportunity. Although the teacher may have designed a particular material to stimulate patterning, the children may be using it to construct other concepts.

How can teachers help children recognize patterns?

Many children quickly grasp the idea of a simple pattern once the teacher draws attention to it. For children who do not easily see pattern relationships, the teacher may wish to rhythmically chant the pattern. Many preschool and kindergarten teachers have noted that this method is very helpful for some children. Perhaps these children can more easily process information that is auditory rather than visual. Patterning activities in the music area may be especially appropriate for these children.

What is symmetry?

Symmetry refers to a similarity of form, arrangement, or design on either side of a dividing line or around a point. There are several types of symmetry. **Reflective symmetry** and **rotational symmetry** are the two types discussed in this book since they can be explored with children.

Reflective symmetry refers to images in which half of the image looks exactly like the other half, but in reverse order. An imaginary line, or axis, divides the two mirror images. The human body is an example of reflective symmetry. The left side of the body is essentially a mirror image of the right side.

Rotational symmetry means that when an object is rotated a specified number of degrees, it looks exactly the same as before it was turned. If a square is rotated 90°, it looks the same as when it was in its original position; however, a rectangle must be rotated 180° before it looks the same. A circle can be turned any number of degrees and still look the same. All are rotationally symmetrical. Starfish, daisies, and sand dollars are objects in nature that are rotationally symmetrical.

Why is it important to explore symmetry with children?

Exploring symmetry is another way to help children develop a deeper understanding of mathematical relationships. As with patterns, in order to perceive symmetry in an object, children must view the individual components in relationship to one another. Only then does the symmetry become apparent. Young children have difficulty thinking about parts in relationship to the whole. Activities that help them to focus on symmetry also advance their ability to deal with part-whole relationships.

How can teachers help children explore reflective symmetry?

Teachers can provide materials that are reflectively symmetrical, such as dolls or butterflies, for children to examine. Teachers can also encourage children to create reflectively symmetrical images and structures with art and building materials. Ink blot designs, or fold-over paintings (activity 2.16), are familiar examples of art projects that allow children to explore reflective symmetry. By building with blocks in front of mirrors (activity 2.17), children can view symmetrical images of their block structures. Activity 2.14 gives suggestions of natural objects that illustrate reflective symmetry and provides ideas for displaying the materials and discussing them with children.

How can teachers help children explore rotational symmetry?

Teachers and children can explore items from nature that are rotationally symmetrical. Pine cones, eucalyptus pods, and sunflowers are examples. Teachers can also select manipulative materials that allow children to experiment with rotational symmetry. Shape sorters, kaleidoscopes, and gears help children deal with concepts of rotational symmetry. Activities 2.15 and 2.18 give ideas for exploring rotational symmetry with children.

How can teachers assess children's understanding of patterns and symmetry?

Teachers can record anecdotal notes of children's comments and explorations of patterns and symmetry. They can also save photographs or examples of their work. Some teachers keep an assessment folder for each child in their class. This provides a space for both written records and student work samples. Other teachers divide a loose-leaf notebook into sections for each child. Pocket dividers hold examples of each child's work so that teachers can chart their progress throughout the year. Documentation panels displayed in the classroom, with photographs of the children's work and transcriptions of their comments about it, may encourage children to revisit and reflect on patterns they have previously created.

Patterning Activities

2.1 Ice-Cream Cones
Manipulative Area

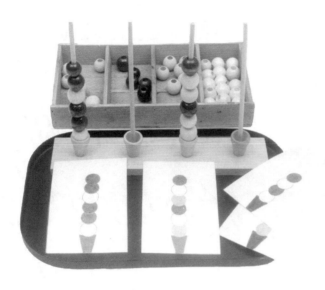

Description
For this activity, children create ice-cream cone patterns by placing macramé beads on dowel frames. Small wooden flowerpots form the cones. The beads are painted the colors of ice-cream flavors. Children can select a pattern card and re-create the pattern or create their own patterns.

Materials
▲ dowel frame, made by drilling four ¼-inch holes in a wooden base (12 by 2 inches) and gluing 9-inch lengths of ¼-inch diameter dowels into the holes
▲ small wooden flowerpots, with holes drilled in the bottoms so they fit onto the dowels
▲ assortment of large-hole macramé beads, painted ice-cream flavor colors with acrylic paint
▲ pattern cards, made by coloring ice-cream cones on note cards and laminating (the scoops of ice cream form the pattern)

Child's Level
This activity is appropriate for both preschool and kindergarten children.

What to Look For
Children will use the macramé beads to re-create and extend the patterns on the cards.
Children will use the beads to create new patterns.
Some children may sort the beads by color.
Some children, particularly the younger ones, may use the beads to create ice-cream cones without regard to pattern.
Some children will quantify the number of ice-cream scoops on their cones.

Modification

Start with simple patterns, such as two colors that alternate. As children become more adept at recognizing patterns, increase the complexity of the patterns on the cards by using more colors and repeating some colors. (*Strawberry–chocolate–chocolate–vanilla, strawberry–chocolate–chocolate–vanilla* is an example of a more difficult pattern.) Older children may wish to create their own pattern cards.

Questions to Extend Thinking

How will you decide which ice-cream flavors to put on the cone?
Can you tell Elijah what the pattern is on your ice-cream cone?
What flavor should I add next to make this pattern?
Can you make up your own ice-cream cone pattern?

Integrated Curriculum Activities

Set up an ice-cream parlor in the dramatic play area (see activity 1.5).
Graph the children's favorite ice-cream flavors (see *More Than Counting,* activity 6.2).
Sing ice-cream songs (see *More Than Singing,* activity 4.2).
Read the poem "Bleezer's Ice Cream," from *The New Kid on the Block,* by Jack Prelutsky (New York: Greenwillow, 1984) to the children. They can make up their own crazy ice-cream flavors.

2.2 Barrettes on Braids
Manipulative or Dramatic Play Area

Description
A small doll with long braids and a basket of selected barrettes inspires patterning in this manipulative activity. Children can place the barrettes in patterns on the braids to show their friends.

Materials
▲ small doll with long braids
▲ barrettes (several colors)

Child's Level
This activity is most appropriate for older preschool or kindergarten children, who can more easily manipulate the barrettes.

What to Look For
Children will form patterns with the barrettes, especially if this is initially modeled or suggested as a possibility.
Some children will try to copy other children's patterns.

Some children will quantify the barrettes or compare the number of barrettes on each braid.

Some children will put the barrettes on the dolls without regard to pattern. They may later begin to form patterns after observing other children.

Modifications

Start with two colors of barrettes for children who are in the initial stages of patterning. This encourages them to form alternating patterns.

Add additional colors or types of barrettes for more experienced patterners. Use leading questions to inspire a variety of patterns.

Questions to Extend Thinking

How can you use these barrettes to form a pattern?

Can you make a pattern with three colors?

What color should I add next to continue Max's pattern?

Can you explain your pattern to Drew?

Is there a way to write down this pattern so we can remember it?

Integrated Curriculum Activities

Add a beauty parlor to the dramatic play area.

As a follow-up activity, put a collection of barrettes for sorting and classifying in the manipulative area (see *More Than Counting*, chapter 3, for information on collections).

Most dolls do not come with long braids. You can add braids to an existing doll by braiding yarn and sewing it to the doll's head.

$\mathcal{2.3}$ Halloween Pattern Strips
Manipulative Area

Description

Teachers create pattern strips for this activity by gluing pumpkin, jack-o'-lantern, and black cat shapes onto poster board strips. Children can extend the patterns by adding cards with these shapes to the pattern strips.

Materials

▲ pattern strips, made by gluing pumpkin, jack-o'-lantern, and black cat shapes onto poster board strips (2½ by 22 inches) to form patterns for children to extend

▲ pumpkin, jack-o'-lantern, and black cat shapes (stickers, crepe paper streamers, and wrapping paper are possible sources) glued to 2-inch poster board squares

Child's Level

This activity is appropriate for either preschool or kindergarten children.

What to Look For

Children will use the Halloween cards to extend the patterns on the pattern strips.

Some children will create their own patterns, particularly if some of the cardboard strips are blank.

Some children will match the shape cards to the shapes on the pattern strips but will not be able to continue the patterns.

Modification

Start with two alternating shapes for children who are just beginning to recognize patterns.

Questions to Extend Thinking

What shape should come next on this pattern strip?

How can I tell which card to put next on my pattern strip?

Can you make up your own pattern with these cards?

Integrated Curriculum Activities

Make Halloween grid and path games (see chapters 6 and 7 for information about grid and path games).

Guess what's inside a pumpkin, and then open one to find out.

Estimate how many grooves are on a pumpkin (see activity 3.4).

Sing Halloween songs that are not scary and emphasize the pretend nature of Halloween (see *More Than Singing,* activity 2.16).

Helpful Hints

Draw lines on the pattern strips with white chalk or paint markers to divide them into boxes. This encourages children to put the cards in the boxes and continue the patterns.

2.4 Shell Patterns
Manipulative Area

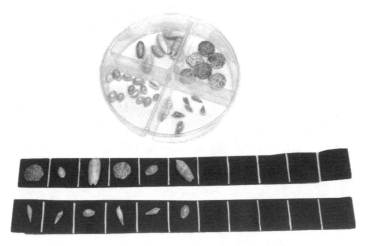

Description
For this activity, children create patterns by placing three types of small seashells onto gridded cardboard strips. Children can work individually or create patterns for a peer to copy or extend.

Materials
▲ 3 types of small seashells
▲ cardboard strips (2½ by 22 inches), with vertical lines drawn every 1½ inches to divide them into boxes

Child's Level
This activity is appropriate for older preschool and kindergarten children.

What to Look For
Children will use the shells to create patterns.
Some children will create patterns for other children to copy.
Some children will put one shell in each box in a one-to-one correspondence relationship without regard to patterning.

Modifications
For children who are just beginning to create patterns, start with just two types of shells. This encourages children to try alternating patterns.
Add more types of shells once children are adept at creating patterns with three types of shells.

Helpful Hints

Look for inexpensive seashells in odd-lot stores, or ask parents for donations. If you have trouble locating small seashells, substitute pasta shells dyed several colors with food coloring.

Comments and Questions to Extend Thinking
Can you use these shells to create a pattern?
I made a pattern with these shells. Can you tell what comes next?
Let's chant the pattern *scallop–scallop–spiral, scallop–scallop–spiral*.

Integrated Curriculum Activities
Use seashells to create imprints in playdough.
Put a beach in the dramatic play area. Fill a child's wading pool with sand and shells.
Scoop shells out of the water table with nets.
Assemble a shell collection for sorting and classifying (see *More Than Counting*, activity 3.8).

2.5 Bingo Marker Patterns
Art Area

Description
Gridded paper and bingo marker paints often suggest the idea of patterning to children. This activity can be added to the art area or used as a special activity.

Materials
▲ bingo marker paints in several colors
▲ 1-inch gridded paper

Child's Level
This activity is appropriate for both preschool and kindergarten children.

What to Look For
Some children will use the bingo markers to create patterns. Alternating colors are common.

Some children will make an entire row of each color.

Some children will use the bingo markers to put one circle in each box in a one-to-one correspondence relationship.

Some children will draw graphic or symmetrical pictures with the markers.

Modification
To encourage patterning with children who are just beginning to recognize patterns, start with just two colors of bingo markers. This often suggests an alternating color pattern to children.

Questions to Extend Thinking
What pattern do you think Becky was thinking of when she made this row?

How many different patterns do you think we could make with these markers?

Is there a way to make the pattern go up and down as well as across the paper?

How did you decide which colors to use?

Integrated Curriculum Activity
Set up the art shelves to focus on circles. Include circular paper and round collage materials, such as bottle caps (see *More Than Painting*, activity 2.11).

Helpful Hints
Wet the sponge top of the bingo marker if the paint does not come out at first.

2.6 Heart and Star Links
Manipulative Area

Description

This inexpensive manipulative material encourages children to create patterns. The colorful plastic hearts and stars link together. Sample pattern cards encourage children to think about patterns as they link the hearts and stars.

Materials

▲ plastic heart and star links, in 1 or 2 colors
▲ pattern cards, made by tracing hearts and stars onto white poster board and laminating

Child's Level

This activity is most appropriate for older preschool and kindergarten children, who can more easily manipulate the linking hearts and stars. Younger children tend to use this material more as a manipulative toy than as a patterning tool.

What to Look For

Children will copy the pattern cards to form patterns with the linking hearts and stars.

Children will create their own patterns with the hearts and stars.

Some children will lay the hearts and stars on top of the shapes on the pattern cards.

Some children will link the hearts and stars without regard for creating a pattern. They may create patterns at a later time after observing other children.

Modification

For children who are just beginning to create patterns, start with either the hearts or the stars, but not both. It is difficult for young children to think about both color and shape at the same time, especially when they are also trying to create pattern relationships.

Questions to Extend Thinking

How can you tell which link to put on next?
Can you make up a pattern with these links?
Do you want to copy this pattern so that you can remember it?

Integrated Curriculum Activities

Use heart and star cookie cutters as printing tools
  (see activity 2.10).
Include heart- and star-shaped paper in the writing area.
Paint with heart- and star-shaped sponges.

Helpful Hints

Look for linking toys in party and carnival supply catalogs or stores.

2.7 Ring Patterns
Manipulative Area

Description

In this activity, children can experiment with creating patterns as they add novelty rings to the fingers of a stuffed glove. The glove is mounted on a wooden stand, which supports it while children manipulate the rings.

Materials

- ▲ child's glove, stuffed with polyester batting
- ▲ frame to hold the glove, made by drilling a ½-inch hole in a wooden base (4 by 5 inches), gluing a 4-inch length of ½-inch diameter dowel into the hole, and tying the glove to the dowel
- ▲ novelty rings, in assorted colors and styles

Child's Level
This activity is most appropriate for older preschool and kindergarten children.

What to Look For
Children will create patterns with the rings, especially if this has been modeled or suggested.

Many children will alternate the colors to create patterns.

Some children will put the rings on the fingers without regard to patterning. They may explore patterns at another time.

Some children will copy other children's patterns.

Some children will quantify the rings on each finger.

Modifications
Simplify the activity by only using two colors of rings. This encourages children to try alternating patterns. Later, additional colors can be added.

To increase the complexity of the activity, introduce other types of rings. This provides children with additional attributes to consider when formulating patterns.

Questions to Extend Thinking
Can you use these rings to create a pattern?

What ring should come next on this finger?

Can you think of a different pattern we could make with the rings?

Integrated Curriculum Activities
Read the book *Grandma's Jewelry Box,* by Linda Milstein (New York: Random House, 1992).

Include sequins and glitter as collage material in the art area.

Ask the children to estimate how many rings will fit on each finger (activity 3.8).

Helpful Hints

Party supply stores are a good source of inexpensive novelty rings, as well as lace gloves, such as the one pictured.

2.8 Sunbonnet Patterns
Manipulative or Dramatic Play Area

Description
In this activity, children insert small artificial flowers into the hatband on a straw sunbonnet to create patterns. Teachers can model patterning with the flowers and encourage children to create their own patterns.

Materials
▲ straw bonnet, with hatband
▲ several types of small artificial flowers

Child's Level
This activity is most appropriate for older preschool or kindergarten children.

What to Look For
Children will create patterns as they decorate the sunbonnet with flowers.

Children will copy each other's patterns.

Children will discuss the patterns they have made.

Some children will want to wear the sunbonnet. Teachers should decide ahead of time how to handle this issue. If teachers have several hats, children could decorate them and then wear them in the dramatic play area.

Some children will insert flowers in the hatband without regard to pattern. They may create patterns at a later time after watching other children.

Modifications
Start with two types of flowers for children who are just beginning to create patterns.
Add additional flowers when children are ready to create more complex patterns.

Questions to Extend Thinking
What order shall we put the flowers in for this sunbonnet?
Can you use the flowers to create a pattern?
How can we tell which flower to put in next?
Can you create a different pattern with the same flowers?

Integrated Curriculum Activities
Assemble a collection of tiny hats for sorting and classifying (see *More Than Counting,* activity 3.4).
Include books about hats in the reading area. *Aunt Flossie's Hats,* by Elizabeth Fitzgerald Howard (New York: Clarion, 1991), *Hats, Hats, Hats,* by Ann Morris (New York: Lothrop, 1989), and *Caps for Sale,* by Esphyr Slobodkina (Reading, MA: Addison-Wesley, 1968) are examples.
Graph the children's hats, perhaps by color one day and type on another day.
Set up a hat shop in the dramatic play area (activity 1.3).

Helpful Hints

Separate the flowers by color or type in a divided container. A silverware caddie works well. This encourages children to notice the similarities and differences among the flowers, which is a necessary first step before patterning.

2.9 Tool Box Patterns
Manipulative Area

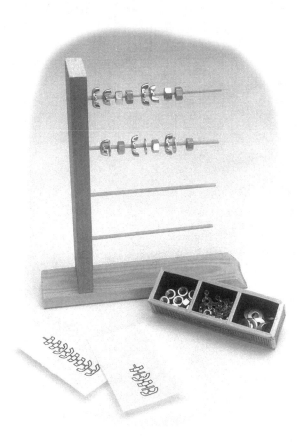

Description
Children place wing nuts, washers, and hexagonal nuts onto a dowel frame to create a variety of patterns with this activity. Sample pattern cards may help children get started.

Materials
▲ wing nuts, washers, and hexagonal nuts (6 or more of each to ensure that there are enough to create patterns)

▲ dowel frame, made by drilling four ³/₁₆-inch diameter holes in a wooden base (approximately 12 by 2 inches), gluing 7-inch-long pieces of ³/₁₆-inch diameter dowels into the holes, and mounting the frame vertically on another piece of wood (also 12 by 2 inches)

▲ pattern cards, made by drawing wing nut, washer, and hexagonal nut shapes onto note cards to form sample patterns

Child's Level

This activity is most appropriate for older preschool and kindergarten children, who can manipulate the small nuts and washers and will not put objects in their mouths.

What to Look For

Children will use the nuts and washers to copy patterns from the pattern cards.

Children will create their own patterns with the nuts and washers.

Some children will sort the nuts and bolts by type rather than create patterns. They may create patterns later after observing other children.

Modifications

Start with just wing nuts and washers for children who are just beginning to create patterns.

Add additional types of nuts and washers for more advanced children.

Questions to Extend Thinking

Can you copy the pattern on this card with these nuts and washers?

What comes next on Julie's pattern?

Is there another pattern we could make?

Integrated Curriculum Activities

Put a construction site in the dramatic play area.

Include woodworking as a class activity if appropriate for your group. Children can hammer nails into wood and turn screws with screw drivers.

Read woodworking books such as *Tools,* by Venice Stone (New York: Scholastic, 1990).

Design math games related to a construction topic (activities 6.8, 7.8a, and 7.8b).

Helpful Hints

Be sure the nuts and washers have holes large enough to fit over the dowels.

2.10 Big and Little Cookie Cutters
Art Area

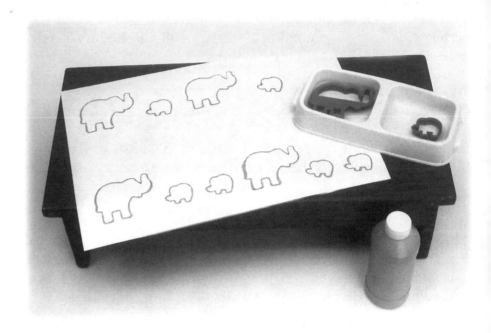

Description

The art area is another part of the classroom that is ideal for encouraging patterning. Big and small cookie cutters of the same shape used as printing tools with paint naturally inspire children to create patterns. Children are especially likely to create patterns with art materials if they are exploring patterns throughout the classroom. Animal cookie cutters often inspire children to create family patterns, such as mother–baby–mother–baby.

Materials
▲ 2 sizes of the same shape of cookie cutter
▲ tempera paint
▲ white construction paper (12 by 18 inches)

Child's Level

This activity is appropriate for both preschool and kindergarten children.

What to Look For

Children will dip the cookie cutters into the paint and observe the images they produce on the paper.

After they know what to expect from the cookie cutters and the paint, some children will begin to produce patterns with the cookie cutters.

Many children will create alternating *big–little* patterns with the cookie cutters.

Modification

More advanced children may want to create patterns with a variety of shapes and sizes of cookie cutters and with different colors of paint.

Comments and Questions to Extend Thinking

If you put one baby elephant after each big elephant, will it make a pattern?

What kind of pattern do you get if you put two baby elephants after each big elephant?

Look! Alice put one little elephant inside each big elephant.

Integrated Curriculum Activities

Use the same cookie cutters with playdough on another day.

Put animal families in the block area (activity 1.7). Children may also create patterns with them.

A sponge in the bottom of the paint container helps keep the paint from dripping when children dip the cookie cutters into it.

2.11 Stringing Straws and Pasta Wheels
Art Area

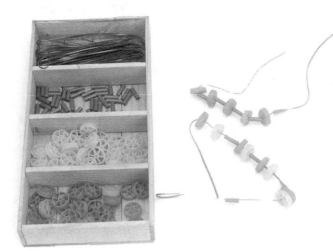

Description

Teachers often observe children creating patterns with stringing activities, particularly if there are just two or three colors or types of objects to string. This activity combines straws, cut into pieces, and pasta wheels. Children often start by alternating the two materials, thus producing simple patterns.

Materials

▲ straw pieces, approximately ½ inch long
▲ colored pasta wheels
▲ plastic cord for stringing

Child's Level

This activity is most appropriate for older preschool or kindergarten children. Although younger children may enjoy stringing the materials, they are less likely to consider the patterning possibilities than older children.

What to Look For

Children may alternate the straws and pasta wheels to create a pattern.

Children may use the materials to make a variety of types of patterns.

Some children will start a pattern but lose track of the pattern as they continue their project.

Some children will use the materials for stringing but not patterning. They may begin to create patterns at a later time after watching other children or listening to their discussions.

Modifications

Start with just one color of straw and one color of pasta for children who are just beginning to create patterns. Varying both color and type of stringing materials may distract them from thinking about patterns.

Add additional types of pasta to challenge children who are experienced with creating patterns.

Questions to Extend Thinking

How could we use these materials to create patterns?

Can you tell what will come next on Tommy's string?

Could we make a pattern if we used just the straws?

Will you make the same pattern or a different pattern for your next necklace?

Integrated Curriculum Activities

Include stringing materials in the manipulative area. Children may use them to create additional patterns.

Place the stringing materials on the art shelf after they have been used for a special activity. This will give children the opportunity to continue creating patterns over an extended period of time.

Helpful Hints

Straws can be easily cut with scissors.

Color the pasta with a mixture of food coloring and rubbing alcohol. The alcohol makes the pasta dry quickly.

2.12 Chanting Patterns–
Pizza Toppings
Music Area

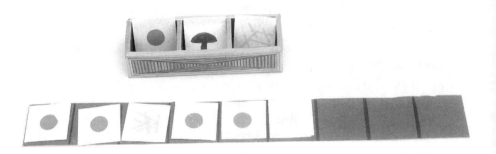

Description
Teachers often find that rhythmically chanting a pattern helps children who are having difficulty in recognizing patterns to more easily perceive them. For this activity, teachers or children can create patterns using pizza topping cutouts. They can then chant the patterns. This activity can be used individually or at group time.

Materials
▲ paper cutouts of pizza toppings (cheese, pepperoni, and mushrooms), mounted on white note cards cut in 2-inch squares
▲ poster board strips (2½ by 18 inches) with lines drawn every 2 inches to create boxes for the pizza toppings

Child's Level
This activity is most appropriate for older preschool and kindergarten children.

What to Look For

Many children will quickly grasp the patterns once they hear them chanted.

Children will create a variety of patterns with the pizza topping cutouts.

Some children will place one pizza topping cutout in each box of the gridded strip in a one-to-one correspondence relationship, without regard to patterning. They may begin to create patterns later after they have had more experience hearing patterns chanted.

Modifications

Start with two choices of pizza toppings with children who are just beginning to recognize patterns.

Kindergarten children may wish to make additional pizza topping cutouts to include in the activity. They may want to preserve their patterns by copying them onto gridded paper strips.

Comments and Questions to Extend Thinking

Let's see if we can chant Peg's pattern.

Can you tell what will come next in my pattern?

What's another pattern we could make?

Can we make a pattern with just mushrooms and pepperoni?

Integrated Curriculum Activities

Make pizza with the children.

Graph the children's favorite pizza toppings (see *More Than Counting*, chapter 6, for information about graphs).

Change the dramatic play area into a pizza parlor.

Read books about pizza, such as *The Lady with the Alligator Purse*, by Nadine Bernard Westcott (Boston: Little, Brown, 1988) and *Pizza Party*, by Grace Maccarone (New York: Scholastic, 1994).

Invite the parents to a class pizza party.

Combine the rhythms of the words for pizza toppings for a music activity (see *More Than Singing*, activity 3.13).

Helpful Hints

Mount the pizza topping cutouts on note cards or poster board squares and laminate for greater durability. Be sure the squares will fit into the boxes on the gridded strips.

If you don't want to draw pizza toppings, cut pictures of toppings from boxes of frozen pizza.

2.13 Can Band Music Patterns

Music Area

Description

Music is filled with patterns, so the music area is a logical part of the classroom for children to explore patterns. This activity includes a variety of sizes of empty cans and a wooden mallet for striking them. Each size of can has a different pitch. The can band seems to naturally foster patterning as children compare the sounds of the cans. Teachers can also create patterns for children to try to recognize or reproduce on the various sizes of cans.

Materials
▲ several sizes of empty aluminum cans
▲ wooden mallet, made by gluing a macramé bead onto a 7-inch-long dowel that has the same diameter as the hole in the bead

Child's Level
This activity is appropriate for either preschool or kindergarten children.

Helpful Hints

The cans can be painted or covered with contact paper to make them more attractive. If you decide to color the cans, make them all the same color so that children do not think that the differences in pitch are due to the color of the can.

What to Look For

Children will experiment with the cans to see how they sound.

As children go back and forth between cans to compare the sounds, patterns will emerge. The teacher can point out the patterns.

Children will create a variety of types of patterns once they recognize the patterning possibilities of the cans.

Modifications

Start with one big can and one small can for children who are just beginning to recognize patterns.

Children may wish to tape-record their patterns. They can listen to each other's patterns and try to reproduce them.

Comments and Questions to Extend Thinking

Listen to the pattern I can play on these two cans.

Can you make up your own pattern with the cans?

If I keep playing each can twice, is that a pattern?

Can you tell what comes next in this pattern?

Integrated Curriculum Activities

Include several sizes of other types of instruments in the music area throughout the year. Use one type of instrument at a time so that children can focus on the pitch variations caused by altering the size of the instrument. (See *More Than Singing,* chapter 5, and *More Than Magnets,* chapter 6, for many ideas).

Play recordings of steel drum music. Children can listen for patterns.

2.14 Reflective Symmetry in Nature
Science Area

Description
Patterns and symmetry occur throughout nature. In this activity, children look for reflective symmetry in items from nature, including seashells, leaves, crabs, and butterflies.

Materials
▲ bivalve seashells (clams, scallops)
▲ leaves, pressed inside a book or ironed between wax paper sheets to keep them from withering
▲ small plastic crabs or lobsters
▲ butterflies or butterfly cutouts

Child's Level
This activity is most appropriate for older preschool or kindergarten children. While younger children may be interested in exploring the materials, they may not yet be ready to focus on symmetry.

Helpful Hints
Bivalve seashells often come apart when children handle them. Try gluing some bivalve seashells onto wood or cardboard so that children can more easily observe the symmetry.

What to Look For

Children will explore the materials and discuss how they look and feel.

Some children will recognize the symmetrical design of the objects.

Some children will represent the objects by drawing them or begin to draw other symmetrical figures.

Modifications

Add additional objects that are reflectively symmetrical once children have explored the original set of materials.

Include objects that are not reflectively symmetrical for comparison purposes. Conch shells and snail shells are not reflectively symmetrical.

Comments and Questions to Extend Thinking

How do these things look?

Is there any part of this leaf that looks like another part of the leaf?

I noticed when you folded the butterfly's wings, they fit exactly together.

Do the two parts of the shell fit together?

Is there any part of your body that is exactly like another part?

Integrated Curriculum Activities

Create rubbings of the leaves by covering them with a thin piece of paper and rubbing over them with the side of a crayon.

Include shells, leaves, and flower petals as collage materials on the art shelves.

Add books with pictures of shells, leaves, and flowers to the reading area.

Take a nature walk with the children and look for objects that are reflectively symmetrical.

Cut fruits in half vertically and observe the symmetry between the two parts with the children. Apples, oranges, and avocados work well.

2.15 Rotational Symmetry in Nature

Science Area

Description
Many objects in nature are rotationally symmetrical. This means that as you turn them, they pass through positions where they look the same as when in their original position. For example, if you hold a starfish so that one arm points upward and gradually rotate it, each time another arm points upward the starfish looks the same as when you started. In this activity, items from nature that are rotationally symmetrical are placed in the science area for children to explore.

Materials
▲ sand dollars
▲ daisies, sunflowers, or similar flowers
▲ eucalyptus pods
▲ starfish

Child's Level
This activity is most appropriate for older preschool or kindergarten children. While younger children may be interested in exploring the materials, they may not yet be ready to focus on symmetry.

What to Look For

Children will handle the objects as they explore them.
Children will rotate the objects as part of their explorations.
Some children will notice that the objects look the same as they
turn them.

Modification

After the children have had ample time to explore the materials,
try adding an outline of the starfish drawn on poster board. This
encourages children to rotate the starfish and try to fit it into the
template. Drawings of other rotationally symmetrical objects,
such as the eucalyptus pod, may encourage children to rotate
them until they look like the drawing.

Questions to Extend Thinking

How does the daisy look as you turn it?
How much do you have to turn the sand dollar before the star
shape points upward again?
Do you notice any similarities between the sand dollar and the
eucalyptus pod?
What other things could we put on the science shelf that would
look the same as we turn them?

Integrated Curriculum Activities

Introduce pinwheels in the outside area. They are rotationally
symmetrical.
Use the materials from this activity to make impressions in playdough. Children can rotate the objects until they fit the molds
created in the playdough.
Add shape sorters to the manipulative area. Children must rotate
the shapes to fit them into the compartments.
Take a nature walk with the children and look for objects that are
rotationally symmetrical. Many flowers are.

Helpful Hints

Small flowers, such as
daisies, can be pre-
served by placing them
between two pieces of
wax paper and ironing
them.

2.16 Fold-Over Painting
Art Area

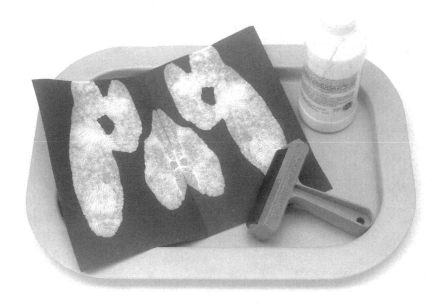

Description
Children are fascinated with the symmetrical designs they can create with this activity. Start by folding dark-colored paper in half and then opening it. Children apply small amounts of white paint to one side of the paper, fold the paper over the paint, and rub the paper with their hands or a paint roller. As they open the paper, a symmetrical design appears. Children love describing what the various designs look like.

Materials
▲ black or dark blue construction paper (12 by 18 inches)
▲ white tempera paint
▲ paint roller (optional)

Child's Level
This activity is appropriate for both preschool and kindergarten children.

What to Look For

Children eagerly apply the paint and are quite excited by the fanciful shapes that emerge.

Many children will notice the symmetrical relationship between the two sides of the paper.

Many children will name their artwork.

Some children will experiment by applying the paint to different parts of the paper and observing the results.

Modification

After children have created designs using white paint on black paper, switch to several colors of paint on white paper. Children can observe that the colors of paint, as well as the shapes created, form a symmetrical pattern.

Comments and Questions to Extend Thinking

Do you see this shape anywhere else on your paper?

Do the two sides look the same or different?

The part you called an "arm" points this way on this side of the paper, and it points the other direction on the other side of the paper.

What did you do to make the two sides symmetrical?

Integrated Curriculum Activities

Read the book *It Looked Like Spilt Milk,* by Charles G. Shaw (New York: Harper, 1993). The shapes in the book resemble the designs created by children in this activity.

Make body tracings of the children by having them lie down on butcher paper while you trace around them. Children can look for symmetry in the outlines.

Encourage interested children to create snow or sand angels (depending on the weather!) by lying on their backs in the snow or sand and moving their arms and legs back and forth. They can then look at the symmetrical images they have created.

Apply the paint with a small spoon. Otherwise, children squirt too much paint onto the paper and it oozes out the sides when the paper is folded over.

2.17 Blocks and Mirrors
Block Area

Description
Mirrors allow children to observe symmetrical images of their own creations, such as block structures or drawings. In this activity, children build with colored table blocks in front of a nonbreakable mirror. The mirror creates a symmetrical image of the block structure. Children quickly notice that the back of their structure appears to be the front in the mirror image.

Materials
▲ colored table blocks, or other small building materials
▲ nonbreakable mirror, to place behind the building area
▲ additional small nonbreakable mirrors, to create images of various angles of the block structures (optional)

Child's Level
This activity is most appropriate for older preschool or kindergarten children.

What to Look For
Children will marvel at the symmetrical image of their work created by the mirror.

Children will notice that the image in the mirror appears to be the reverse of their structure, so that the back now appears to be the front.

Children will add detail to their block structures in order to see how they appear in the mirror.

Modification

Add additional mirrors placed at angles around the area where the child is building. This allows children to view their block structures from several angles.

Questions to Extend Thinking

Does the block structure in the mirror look just like your block structure?

What will happen to the mirror image if you put another block on this side?

If you add a block to the back of your building, will it be on the back or the front of the building in the mirror?

Can you find this part of the building in the mirror?

Integrated Curriculum Activities

Allow children to draw in front of small mirrors. They can observe the symmetry created by the mirrors and watch changes emerge as they continue to draw.

Add large, nonbreakable mirrors, such as are often used in dramatic play, or large reflective paper to the block area. Children can observe symmetrical images of large block structures. They may also notice the anomaly of the reflected image, which causes the back of the block structure to appear to be the front.

Helpful Hints

For inexpensive, unbreakable mirrors, try school locker mirrors.

2.18 Symmetry with Kaleidoscopes
Science Area

Description
Kaleidoscopes provide a marvelous means for children to observe rotational symmetry. The mirrors inside create a three-part symmetrical image centering around a point. The kaleidoscope also creates multiple copies of this image. As children turn the kaleidoscope, they can observe a vast array of symmetrical forms partially determined by the way they arrange objects in the kaleidoscope. From an educational standpoint, the most useful kaleidoscopes are those that allow children to directly place objects in the kaleidoscope, as opposed to kaleidoscopes that are sealed.

Materials
▲ several kaleidoscopes, designed so that children can place objects directly in the kaleidoscope
▲ a variety of materials to place in the kaleidoscopes (shape cutouts, ribbon pieces, beads, small shells, etc.)
▲ observational notepad, where children can record or dictate their observations or draw representations of the images they see in the kaleidoscopes (optional)

Child's Level
This activity is most appropriate for older preschool or kindergarten children.

What to Look For

Children will place objects in the kaleidoscopes and observe how
   they look.
Children will be excited by the way the kaleidoscopes alter the
   images of the objects.
Some children will notice the symmetry in the images created.
Children will notice that the same image appears many times
   when viewed through a kaleidoscope.
Children will discuss and describe what they see.
Some children will try to re-create the images.

Modification

Start with just one type of material to place in the kaleidoscopes.
Children may become overwhelmed if there are too many choices
of accessory materials. This may distract them from carefully
observing the kaleidoscopic images. Shape cutouts are good to
begin with since children can clearly see how the shapes change
when viewed through the kaleidoscope.

Questions to Extend Thinking

What do you see in the kaleidoscope?
Does the circle still look like a circle?
What happens when you turn the kaleidoscope?
Do any parts look the same?
Can you draw what you see in the kaleidoscope?

Integrated Curriculum Activities

Let children draw images to view through a kaleidoscope.
Observe objects in the classroom through a prism.
Compare how objects look through prisms with different types of
   cut glass.

Helpful Hints

Some kaleidoscopes
come with colorful
shapes to view. Other-
wise, you can use shape
hole punches to quickly
produce shapes for use
with the kaleidoscopes.

2.19 Guess the Pattern
Group Time

Description

In this game, which is intended primarily for kindergarten, the teacher creates patterns with the children's shoes. The children try to figure out the teacher's pattern. There are endless variations of this game. Some possibilities are:

brown–white, brown–white
sneaker–sandal–sandal, sneaker–sandal–sandal
shoe pointing up–shoe pointing down,
shoe pointing up–shoe pointing down

Material

▲ shoes from the children in the class (temporarily borrowed during group time)

Child's Level

This activity is most appropriate for kindergarten children.

What to Look For

Children will eagerly attempt to deduce the patterns created in this game.

Children will become more skilled at recognizing patterns with experience, and will also think of more pattern possibilities.

Some children will begin to create their own shoe patterns after playing this game.

For many children, patterns that alternate two items will be the easiest to recognize.

Modification

Once children have become experienced at figuring out patterns created by the teacher, let them take turns at creating patterns for the rest of the class to recognize.

Questions to Extend Thinking

Can you tell what kind of shoe should come next?

What kind of pattern could I make with these buckle and tie shoes?

Can the direction the shoes are facing make a pattern?

Does anyone have an idea for another pattern?

Integrated Curriculum Activities

Put a collection of small novelty shoes in the manipulative area for sorting and classifying (see *More Than Counting*, activity 3.3).

Graph the children's shoes, perhaps by color one day and by another attribute, such as type of fastener, on another day (see *More Than Counting*, activity 6.3).

Set up a shoe store in the dramatic play area (activity 1.4).

Have children remove just one shoe. Then you can match the shoes to their mates and avoid mix-ups when returning the shoes to the children.

Estimation

Stephen ran to his teacher as soon as he entered the classroom. He opened his hand to show her five apple seeds. During lunch the day before, the children had guessed how many seeds were in the uncut apples at the table. Even the teacher was surprised when each apple had a different number of seeds. Stephen wanted to show his teacher the seeds he had collected at home. He told her that he had guessed his apple would have seven seeds, the same as the one at his lunch table. In fact, his apple had only five seeds.

▲ ▲ ▲

At group time, the teacher asked the children to estimate how many buckeye nuts were inside a small, clear jar. The group of children ranged in age from three to five years. Bonnie, age three, guessed the same number of buckeyes as her age, as did Rachel. Marisela, age four, estimated twelve, which was as high as she could rote count. Daniel, age four and a half, estimated ten. Aloke, age five, estimated 100. There were actually seventeen buckeyes in the jar. The children all agreed that counting was the best way to find out how many were really in the jar.

▲ ▲ ▲

Children enjoy guessing games from an early age—for example, guessing which hand behind Grandpa's back holds the treat. They delight in hiding, sometimes in plain view, and giggle as the adult guesses where they are hiding, until they squeal and say, "Here I am!" Young children, however, rarely think about estimating, or guessing how many, until someone introduces the possibility. For this reason, teachers need to plan inviting estimation activities, based on topics of interest to children, and take advantage of naturally occurring experiences, such as guessing how many seeds are in a piece of fruit or how many blocks are needed to make a car.

Teachers' Questions
What is estimation?

Estimation is the approximation of a quantity without counting. It is a judgment or opinion that is based on information already available. For example, children may estimate how many small buttons are in a jar by relying on previous knowledge of how many large buttons were in the same jar. They may estimate the number of seeds in an orange based on previous knowledge of how many seeds were in an apple.

Why is estimation an important skill?

"Estimation skills and understanding enhance the abilities of children to deal with everyday quantitative situations," according to The National Council of Teachers of Mathematics. They include estimation as one of the standards for kindergarten through grade twelve. This standard focuses on estimation as a way to help children develop "flexibility in working with numbers and measurements, and an awareness of reasonable results."[1]

Estimation is a time saver, which may be important to both adults and children. For example, teachers might estimate the quantity of construction paper needed for an art activity rather than counting out enough sheets of paper for each child. Children might estimate how many beads of each color they need for a necklace.

Estimation also is necessary to determine a quantity that cannot be counted or is not yet available. School districts may need to estimate the number of preschool children who might attend school in the year 2010. Since those children have not yet been born, the quantity is not yet available and must be estimated. Children might estimate how many muffins they need to bake for a parent luncheon. Since they may not know specifically how many parents plan to attend, they must estimate how many to bake.

Is estimation merely guessing?

Estimation is more than guessing; it is based on some previous knowledge. For example, teachers know from experience that many children want more than one piece of paper for an art activity. They also know that a package contains one hundred sheets of construction paper. Based on this knowledge, they might estimate that about thirty sheets will be needed for a group of fifteen children. Therefore, they may divide the package in half and take a little less to get close to their estimate of thirty sheets of paper.

Children also estimate based on their levels of thinking and prior experiences. For example, if a child brings cookies for a birthday treat, classmates may look at the number of cookies on the tray and speculate about whether there are enough cookies for each person to have one or two. They may remember when other children brought treats to school and try to decide if there are more cookies this time or fewer.

What should teachers expect when they first ask children to estimate?

In many instances, children give illogical answers, especially during initial estimation experiences. Preschool and kindergarten children often guess their age. Older preschool and kindergarten children are interested in very large numbers and may give answers such as one hundred, a zillion, or even infinity. These types of answers are typical of young children due to their preoperational level of thinking and their lack of experience. Kindergarten children are also likely to be swayed by their peers. They may select the same amount as a friend or the same number as the majority of the class. For this reason, teachers may want to solicit estimates from children individually, rather than during group time.

When do children become more logical in estimation?

Children use more logical thinking strategies to estimate after they have had numerous experiences comparing their estimates to actual quantities. They also become more logical in their thinking when they are confronted with answers different from their own. Young children profit from many opportunities to solve problems using their own thinking strategies, but they also benefit when they hear another child's point of view. This forces children to rethink and defend their own point of view, sometimes leading to disequilibrium or new learning.

How can teachers encourage children to estimate?

Teachers can plan interesting estimation activities as well as stimulate interest in estimation as part of natural experiences throughout the day. Specific activities planned by the teacher may highlight estimation as a possible method of determining quantity. Activities that coordinate with the rest of the curriculum or build on the interests of the children are particularly effective. For example, if a class has recently visited a pumpkin farm, the children might be interested in estimating how many grooves are on a pumpkin (activity 3.4). Other opportunities for estimation arise as children use the materials in the classroom. For example, the teacher may suggest that children estimate how many marbles will sink a boat in the sensory table (activity 3.9), how many cookies will fit into a jar in the dramatic play area (activity 3.7), or how many pieces of tape are needed to secure two pieces of paper together.

What types of estimation activities can teachers plan?

Teachers can plan estimation activities that focus attention on an existing quantity, spatial relationships, or an as yet unknown quantity. Estimation activities often involve an existing quantity, such as the number of pacifiers in a jar (activity 3.1). Estimation activities may relate to spatial relationships, such as the number of children who can fit into a T-rex footprint (activity 3.5). Sometimes estimation activities are designed to focus children's attention on a quantity hidden from view, such as the number of seeds in an apple (activity 3.6).

When should teachers introduce estimation activities?

Teachers may initially wish to introduce estimation activities during group time. This seems to encourage children to also think about estimation during the day. Group experiences provide children with opportunities to encounter different opinions and methods of solving a problem. Teachers can also introduce the possibility for estimation in other curriculum areas throughout the day as children interact with materials. For example, children might estimate how many gloves the whole group needs before going outside.

What areas of the classroom provide opportunities for estimation activities?

All areas of the classroom can provide a forum for estimation problems. For example, during group time, children have the opportunity to listen to each other as they estimate how many objects fit in a container. At the lunch or snack table, they may guess how many orange slices are in a bowl. In the dramatic play area, children may estimate how many eggs will fit in a pan and then check to see if their guesses were accurate. When working in the art area, children may estimate how many cotton balls will fit on various pieces of paper or how many pieces of rigatoni are needed for necklaces or bracelets. In the manipulative area, they might speculate about how many snowmen are in a nesting set or how many Duplo blocks it will take to make a tower as tall as they are. Even the sensory table may encourage estimation as children guess how many ice balls will fit in a bottle or how many frogs can sit on a lily pad. Teachers can plan estimation activities for these areas as well as take advantage of daily situations in which children can use estimation to solve problems.

How does estimation relate to science activities?

Children may incorporate estimation into their observations as they closely examine the physical properties of materials. Teachers can encourage estimation through their design of the science area. For example, the teacher might place a sign above a pumpkin that reads, "How many grooves are on the pumpkin? What is your estimate?" (activity 3.4). Paper and pencils might be available to document the answers. Later, during a group activity, the teacher might record each child's estimate and ask the children how to determine the actual quantity of grooves. Many children will suggest counting as a method of comparison. The actual number of grooves on each pumpkin can then be compared to the estimates, providing children with feedback about the accuracy of their estimates.

How does estimation relate to physical-knowledge activities?

Estimation is frequently a component of activities in which children explore the properties of materials, such as weight, volume, and balance. Children can estimate how many bottles they will knock over in a bowling game with various sizes of balls, how many cups of water will fill a bottle, or how many blocks can be stacked before a tower falls over. These types of activities are a common part of the curriculum in preschool and kindergarten programs. Teachers can stimulate interest in estimation through questions that focus children's attention on approximation. Suggested questions are included with each activity.

What should teachers do if children do not grasp the concept of estimation?

Teachers should continue to plan estimation activities for group time. Teachers can also reduce the quantity of objects in estimation activities. Group activities provide opportunities for children to observe the teacher and other children as they model estimation. Group activities allow the teacher to assess the class's understanding of estimation and adjust the quantity of objects in the activity. Smaller quantities of objects, fewer than twenty for preschool children and fifty for kindergarten children, allow children to be more successful when estimating.

How can teachers assess children's estimation abilities?

Group estimation activities provide concrete documentation of children's abilities, since the teacher records individual responses on poster board or chart paper. Teachers can gather documentation from science activities that provide children with the opportunity to record estimates, such as seeds in a sunflower head (activity 3.10). Teachers may also record information about individual children in the form of anecdotal notes on index cards or in a notebook.

ENDNOTES
1. National Council of Teachers of Mathematics, *Curriculum and Evaluation Standards for School Mathematics* (Reston, VA: NCTM, 1989) 38.

Estimation Activities

3.1 How Many Pacifiers?

Description
This activity is a good introduction to the use of estimation to approximate a quantity. Children estimate the number of baby pacifiers in a clear, plastic jar. Later they compare the estimated quantity to the actual number of pacifiers in the jar. This activity coordinates well with a baby unit.

Materials
▲ one 18–ounce clear peanut butter jar with lid
▲ 7 pacifiers

Child's Level
This activity is appropriate for preschool and kindergarten children. It's a good beginning estimation experience because the quantity is small and the objects are large enough so that none of them are hidden from the child's view.

What to Look For
Some children will guess their age.
Some children will guess very large numbers.

Some children will try to count the pacifiers in the jar before
  estimating.
Young or inexperienced children may not give a numerical answer.
  They may just say "pacifiers."
With experience, children will become more accurate in their
  estimates.

Helpful Hints

Do not use pacifiers
with very young children
who may be tempted to
put them in their
mouths as they count to
check the estimation.

Modifications

Use other large objects, such as walnuts, throughout the year to
  coordinate with other units.
For children who have had experience with estimation and are
  ready to work with larger quantities, use tiny pacifiers, such as
  those found in party stores.

Questions to Extend Thinking

How many pacifiers do you think are in this jar?
Is there more than one pacifier in the jar?
How can we find out how many pacifiers are actually in the jar?

Integrated Curriculum Activities

Set up the dramatic play area as a nursery and include
  baby props, such as blankets, bottles, and diapers.
Sing songs about babies, such as "Hurry Mama" (see *More
  Than Singing,* activity 2.9). It encourages children to
  think of things to bring for baby to stop the crying.
Plan a baby-theme group time (see *More Than Singing,*
  activity 8.10).
Design baby-theme math games for your class (activities
  6.9, 7.9a, and 7.9b).

3.2 How Many Bears?

Description

For this activity, children estimate how many papa bear counters will fit into each of three sizes of nesting cups. The teacher can ask estimation questions as the children play. Children may construct the relationship between the size of the container and how many bears it will hold.

Materials

▲ 3 small nesting cups, each a different size
▲ 10 papa teddy bear counters

Child's Level

This activity is appropriate for younger preschool children. The papa bear counters are too large to be a choking hazard. They are of high interest to young children, and the quantity each cup holds is under five.

What to Look For

Some children initially play with the bears in a pretend play manner.

Some children may stack or nest the cups.

Some children will fill each cup with the bears.

Some children will estimate that the same quantity will fit into each cup.

Experienced children will guess that a different quantity will fit into each cup.

Modifications
For variety, use other objects in combination with the nesting cups.

For older children who may be ready to work with larger quantities, use 12-ounce and 18-ounce sizes of clear peanut butter jars in place of the nesting cups.

Questions to Extend Thinking
How many bears do you think you can fit into the red cup?

Do you think the red cup will hold just as many bears as the yellow cup?

Will more than one bear fit into this cup?

Integrated Curriculum Activities
Read books about teddy bears, such as *Corduroy,* by Donald Free-man (New York: Viking, 1968) and *When the Teddy Bears Came,* by Martin Waddell (Cambridge, MA: Candlewick, 1995).

Include varieties of plush teddy bears in the dramatic play area. Encourage children to estimate how many of those bears will fit into the doll bed, for example.

Design teddy bear math games for the class (see *More Than Count-ing,* activities 5.3 and 5.14).

Make an interactive chart to go with the familiar song "Ten in the Bed" (see *More Than Singing,* activity 2.13).

Helpful Hints
Small flocked bears are available in craft stores, if plastic bears are unavailable. Be sure they are large enough to not present a choking hazard.

3.3 Buckeyes or Acorns?

Description

This is a more complex estimation activity in which children must guess the quantities of two different materials, buckeyes and acorns, which are sealed in two identical containers. The jars are placed in the science area during the day for the children to examine. The teacher introduces the estimation activity during a whole group experience and records the results. This activity allows children to compare how the size of the objects placed in a container affects the number that will fit. They learn to vary their estimates accordingly.

Materials

▲ 10 buckeye nuts and 13 acorns
▲ 2 identical clear plastic jars with lids

Child's Level

This activity is appropriate for older preschool and kindergarten children, since they must estimate without manipulating the materials. This requires more abstract thinking. This activity is best introduced after children have had numerous experiences estimating the quantity of one type of object in a single container.

What to Look For

Some children will estimate that each jar holds the same amount, since the jars are the same size.

Some children may focus on the size of the buckeye compared to the size of the acorn and estimate that the jar of buckeyes must contain fewer than the jar of acorns.

Some children may be unable to understand the question of estimation.

Modification

Use only the acorns, but two different sizes of jars, for the estimation activity.

Comments and Questions to Extend Thinking

Do you estimate that more buckeyes or more acorns are in the jar?

How would you tell someone else how to estimate how many nuts are in the jar?

I notice that the acorns are a different size than the buckeyes. Do you think that affects how many can fit inside the jar?

Integrated Curriculum Activities

Display a selection of nuts in the science area.

Place buckeyes, clear jars, and tongs in the sensory table. Ask estimation questions as children explore the materials.

Assemble a collection of nuts for sorting and classifying (see *More Than Counting,* activity 3.15).

Sing songs about nuts (see *More Than Singing,* activity 6.8).

Use nuts as counters or movers for math games (see *More Than Counting,* activities 4.5, 5.7, 5.12, and 5.18).

Helpful Hints

Seal the jars with tape to discourage children from opening them and counting the buckeyes and acorns before the group activity.

Substitute another kind of nut if you don't have buckeyes in your location.

3.4 Grooves on a Pumpkin

Thanks to Nora Cordrey for this idea.

Description

This autumn activity provides opportunities for children to estimate something they could easily count to quantify. It takes great restraint by the children not to do so! The teacher tells the children to estimate whether the pumpkin has about twenty, thirty, or forty grooves. The teacher compiles the information and transfers it to a graph, made with three columns for recording the estimates. This activity requires children to channel their estimates within the confines of three fixed choices.

Materials

▲ 1 large pumpkin
▲ index cards or slips of paper and pencils, for recording the estimations
▲ poster board, for making the sign that encourages children to estimate

Child's Level

This activity is most appropriate for kindergarten children. They will be better able to understand the concept of estimation when given a choice of three quantities. They will also be better able to wait for a longer period of time to compile the results of estimations. The quantity of grooves on the pumpkin is too large for most preschool children; there may be thirty or more grooves. Estimation of grooves is also more abstract than estimation of concrete objects.

Number Stickers

What to Look For

Some children will be unable to withhold the impulse to count instead of estimate.

Some children will guess a quantity other than the three choices.

Some children will pick the amount that has the most votes on the estimation chart.

Some children will change their estimations after observing the results of the estimations of other children.

Modification

For children who need to work with smaller quantities, select a smaller, pumpkin-shaped gourd.

Comments and Questions to Extend Thinking

Do you think there are about twenty, thirty, or forty grooves in the pumpkin?

Bob, you estimated twenty grooves on the pumpkin. How did you decide on that number?

How can we keep track of the grooves that have already been counted?

Integrated Curriculum Activities

Include other pumpkin activities, such as painting pumpkins, scrubbing pumpkins, and scooping seeds out of the inside of a pumpkin.

Read books about pumpkins, such as *Pumpkin Pumpkin,* by Jeanne Titherington (New York: Greenwillow, 1986).

Take a field trip to a pumpkin farm. Before the trip, have children guess where pumpkins grow (on a tree, a vine, a bush, or under the ground) and graph the results (see *More Than Counting,* activity 6.6).

Select a pumpkin with clearly defined grooves that can be accurately quantified by counting and compared to the estimates.

3.5 How Many Fit into a T-Rex Footprint?

Thanks to Michael Benton for this idea.

Description

This activity coordinates with a dinosaur unit. The teacher makes a paper footprint the size of a Tyrannosaurus rex foot. The footprint is placed in the gross-motor area with a sign nearby asking the question, "How many children's feet fit into a T-rex footprint?" Children are naturally curious to find out the answer. The teacher asks them to estimate before they take turns standing inside the print. The teacher traces around each child's feet.

Materials

▲ a large paper outline, to represent the footprint of Tyrannosaurus rex
▲ a teacher or other adult to trace the children's feet inside the print

Child's Level

Estimations such as this are most appropriate for older preschool and kindergarten children. Younger children may have difficulty understanding the concept of how many will fit inside a shape when concrete objects are not used.

What to Look For

Many children will be quite excited to discover how many of their
footprints will fit inside the dinosaur footprint.

Many children will want to stand inside the dinosaur footprint
before estimating the number needed.

Modifications

Teachers may wish to provide opportunities for children to estimate how many will fit inside more conventional shapes, such
as a rectangle or square, before introducing the footprint
activity.

If several classes wish to use the same activity, use masking tape to
create the footprint. Ask children to estimate how many of their
shoes will fit into the footprint. Children can then place their
shoes inside the outline and quantify the result. Since no outline
of the shoes is made, this does not provide a permanent record
of the estimation.

Questions to Extend Thinking

How many of your footprints do you estimate will fit inside the
dinosaur footprint?

How many teacher footprints do you think would fit?

Can you sit inside the dinosaur footprint?

Integrated Curriculum Activities

Include books, such as *If the Dinosaurs Came Back,* by Bernard
Most (New York: Harcourt, 1978), in the reading area.

Put fossils in the science area.

Have children clap the beats in a chant or poem about dinosaurs
or clap the syllables in dinosaur names (see *More Than Singing,*
activities 3.6 and 3.2).

Let children vote on their favorite dinosaur and graph the results.

Put dinosaur word cards in the writing center.

Make a dinosaur math suitcase for children to take home (see
More Than Counting, activity 8.4).

Helpful Hints

The T-rex footprint is
approximately 36 inches
in diameter.

3.6 Lunchtime Guesses

Description

This estimation activity can be planned by the teacher or may occur naturally as children eat lunch or a snack. The teacher asks the children to estimate how many seeds might be inside an apple. The responses can be recorded and compared to the estimates of children at other tables. After the apples have been cut open, the children can verify the estimates. They may want to repeat this activity on other occasions and compare the results. This activity combines science and math and gives children the opportunity to make an educated guess when they cannot see the actual objects they are estimating. By comparing apples, children discover that the contents of materials that appear to be identical may not be exactly the same.

Materials

▲ several apples, so that small groups of children each have an apple to work with
▲ paper and pencil, for recording the children's estimates and the actual quantity of seeds

Child's Level

This activity is appropriate for preschool-age children since the quantity of seeds inside apples is less than seven or eight.

What to Look For

Many children will guess their age at first.

Some children will not be able to venture an estimate because the seeds are not observable.

In subsequent estimations of seeds in an apple, many children will estimate the same amount as in the first experience.

Modifications

Plan the same activity using a different variety of apple. Children can compare the results.

Suggest that children estimate the number of seeds in other fruits, such as oranges, when they are served for lunch.

Comments and Questions to Extend Thinking

Can you estimate how many seeds might be inside the apple before I cut it into slices?

Yesterday the apple had five seeds. Do you think this apple will have more, less, or the same number of seeds?

Do you think this small apple has as many seeds as this big apple?

Integrated Curriculum Activities

Plan other apple activities, such as cooking with apples or using apples as a printing tool.

Use apple cookie cutters with playdough. Children can estimate how many playdough cookies will fit on their tray.

Let children taste three types of apples and graph the results (see *More Than Counting,* activity 6.5).

Design apple path games for the math area (see *More than Counting,* activities 5.11 and 5.22).

Set up a large pulley for children to transport plastic fruits back and forth to one another (see *More Than Counting,* activity 7.12).

Read the book *Apple Trees,* by Gail Saunders-Smith (Mankato, MN: Capstone, 1998) to the class.

Helpful Hints

Use an apple corer for easy access to the seeds inside the apple.

3.7 How Many Cookies in a Jar?

Description

For this activity, children estimate how many of each of three different sizes of cookie will fit into a cookie jar. The best time to plan this activity is during either small or large group experiences since a teacher is needed to organize the activity and record the estimates. Children discover that the size of the cookie affects the quantity that will fit in the jar. They may also find out that the number of cookies that fit depends on how they are packed in the jar.

Materials

▲ 3 different sizes of cookies
▲ small clear cookie jar

Child's Level

This activity is most appropriate for kindergarten children. The inclusion of three different sizes of cookies to estimate and the organization required to complete the steps in the estimation make this activity too complex for preschool children.

What to Look For

Some children may fill the jar with cookies without estimating the quantity that might fit inside.

Some children will spend long periods of time thinking about how many of each type of cookie might fit inside the cookie jar.

Many children may need assistance in keeping track of the estimations and in recording the responses.

Modification

For younger or less experienced children, use one type of cookie for the estimation activity.

Comments and Questions to Extend Thinking

Can you estimate how many big cookies will fit inside the cookie jar?

How many little cookies do you think will fit in the cookie jar?

Julie and Amanda think the jar will hold more of the smaller cookies; Jim thinks the jar will hold more of the larger cookies.

Integrated Curriculum Activities

Read the book *The Doorbell Rang,* by Pat Hutchins (New York: Greenwillow, 1986).

Bake cookies with the class.

Put sifters and colanders in the sensory table with flour and rice (see *More Than Magnets,* activity 4.9).

Sing a quantification song about cookies (activity 5.6).

To help children focus on one-to-one correspondence, use plastic tape to divide a cookie sheet into boxes. Children can use the gridded cookie sheet with magnetic cookies in the dramatic play area (activity 1.1).

Helpful Hints

Cookie magnets can be used instead of real cookies. They are often found in grocery stores.

3.8 How Many Rings?

Description

Children love to place rings on their fingers. For this activity, a small glove is stuffed and tied shut. Children estimate how many rings will fit on each finger. They can then check the results by actually placing rings on the fingers of the glove. The glove from activity 2.7 can also be used for this activity; however, the rings should be uniform in size. This activity gives children an opportunity to observe how the length of the fingers affects how many rings will fit.

Materials

▲ child's glove, stuffed with polyester batting

▲ frame to hold the glove, made by drilling a ½-inch hole in a wooden base (4 by 5 inches), gluing a 4-inch length of ½-inch diameter dowel into the hole, and tying the glove to the dowel

▲ collection of rings, identical in width and large enough to slip easily over the fingers of the glove

Child's Level

This activity is appropriate for older preschool and kindergarten children. Younger children may focus their attention on wearing the rings themselves.

What to Look For

Some children, even older children, may initially wear the rings.

Some children may place the rings onto the fingers of the glove without regard for estimation.

Some children will discuss how many rings will fit onto the fingers and check the results.

Modification

To extend this activity for older children, use an above-the-elbow glove and add bracelets to the collection of jewelry the children use in the estimation activity.

Questions to Extend Thinking

How will you estimate how many rings will fit onto each finger of the glove?

Do you think this finger (pointing to the thumb) or this finger (pointing to the little finger) will hold more rings?

Integrated Curriculum Activities

Include the book *Grandma's Jewelry Box,* by Linda Milstein (New York: Random House, 1992) in the reading area.

Assemble a collection of jewels for sorting and classifying (see *More Than Counting,* activity 3.11).

Use jewelry as counters or movers for math games (see *More Than Counting,* activities 4.12 and 5.9).

Put sequins and glitter in the art area for gluing.

Helpful Hints

Put a different set of rings in the dramatic play area for children who want to use them for dress-up.

3.9 Sink the Boat

Description

This estimation activity can be done in the sensory table. Children estimate how many marbles it will take to sink small boats and then carry out the experiment. This activity combines math and science and helps children construct the relationship between the weight of the marbles and how many it takes to sink the boat. Children learn that estimates can be revised based on observations.

Materials

▲ sensory table or small dishpan, filled with enough water to allow the boats to float
▲ black or dark marbles (about 50)
▲ small plastic or rubber boats (2 per child)
▲ 1 ladle for each child participating in the activity

Child's Level

This activity is appropriate for preschool and kindergarten children. It is not appropriate for children who may still put objects into their mouths.

What to Look For

Some children may ladle the marbles into the boats without regard to estimation.

Some children may communicate to each other about their estimates of how many marbles will sink the boat.

Children will check to see if their estimates are accurate.

Some children will revise their estimates based on their prior observations as they experiment with other boats.

Modifications

Use small plastic teddy bears in place of the marbles. Children will discover that since the bears are lighter in weight, it takes more of them to sink the boats.

For children who are ready to handle larger quantities, use a larger size boat with the marbles.

Comments and Questions to Extend Thinking

How many marbles do you think will sink this boat?

Your boat is still floating. How many more marbles do you estimate you will need to add to sink the boat?

What is happening to the boat as you add more marbles?

Integrated Curriculum Activities

Use the same materials in the outdoor gross-motor area.

Read the predictable book *Who Sank the Boat?* by Pamela Allen (New York: Coward-McCann, 1982).

Design pirate math games for the class (activities 6.3, 7.3a, and 7.3b).

Be sure the boats are deep enough to hold the marbles.

3.10 How Many Seeds Are in the Sunflower Head?

Description

This activity, which combines science and math, allows children to estimate how many seeds are in the head of a sunflower. It is introduced in autumn when the sunflower is fully mature and full of seeds. Some children may also wish to determine approximately how many seeds each child can eat after the seeds are roasted. Children can compare the actual number of seeds in the sunflower to their estimates before the seeds are eaten.

Materials

▲ 1 or more sunflower heads with seeds
▲ paper and pencils, for recording the responses

Child's Level

This activity is most appropriate for kindergarten children. The large quantity of seeds and the sequence of the activity may be too complex for younger children. Kindergarten children are typically very interested in large numbers.

What to Look For

Some children may attempt to count all the seeds.

Some children may estimate a small number rather than a large number.

Some children will guess very large numbers—a million, for example.

Modification

For younger children, use a smaller sunflower head with fewer seeds inside.

Questions to Extend Thinking

About how many seeds do you think are in the sunflower?

If each person can have ten roasted sunflower seeds, do you estimate that this sunflower has enough seeds?

Integrated Curriculum Activities

Include books, such as *Sunflowers,* by Gail Saunders-Smith (Mankato, MN: Capstone, 1998), *Sunflower,* by Miela Ford and Sally Noll (New York: Greenwillow, 1995), and *The Sunflower House,* by Eve Bunting (New York: Harcourt, 1996), in the reading area.

Roast the seeds for eating after the estimation.

Plan ahead and plant the sunflower in the spring. The children can chart the growth of the plant from seed to tall sunflower plant.

Put tweezers and a sunflower in the science area. Children can use the tweezers to pluck the seeds.

Helpful Hints

Check around your area for farmers who grow sunflowers and might be willing to donate several to the school.

Math for Toddlers

Eden, age two years and eight months, sat with a group of four other toddlers at the snack table. The teacher was distributing a mini-muffin to each child. She gave each child one muffin. Eden placed her muffin in one hand, held out the other hand and said, "Two! I am two!"

▲ ▲ ▲

Elias, who would turn three in one month, played in the dramatic play area with dolls and blankets. He carefully placed each of the three dolls in a doll bed and began to place a blanket on each doll. He had only two blankets. He searched all the drawers until he found another blanket for the last doll. "There! Each baby has a blanket."

▲ ▲ ▲

Toddlers depend on teachers and caregivers to create a math-rich environment and supply them with the necessary language to further their development. During this period of greater mobility and explosion in language development, toddlers add the vocabulary of mathematics to their growing communication repertoire. Careful planning of curriculum materials increases the opportunities for the construction of mathematical knowledge at this crucial period of development for young children.

Teachers' Questions
What are the ages of children identified as toddlers?

Child development experts identify the period from one year to three years of age as the toddler stage. The label "toddler" is also used by many state and local child care licensing agencies in order to define teacher-child ratio requirements. Many nursery schools and child care centers group children in this age range into two groups and may identify classrooms as Toddler I and Toddler II.

Are the activities in this chapter for all toddlers?

The activities in this chapter are designed for older toddlers, from about two and a half to three years of age. Younger toddlers are often exploring materials at the sensory-motor level of development. In many instances, the children put the materials into their mouths to explore them. The primary focus of the curriculum for younger toddlers is on the routines of the day, including feeding and diaper-changing. Older toddlers become more independent in self-care, often use language to express themselves, and explore materials in a more mature manner. The toddler period six months prior to the preschool age of three is the most appropriate time to use the activities in this chapter.

Are toddlers interested in math?

Yes! Toddlers are very interested in experiences that allow them to interact with interesting math materials and the adults around them. Two year olds are especially interested in going up and down the steps as an adult counts for them. They also love to play give-and-take games with parents and teachers. Toddlers are proud of being two years old and love to have two of everything.

What characteristics are typical of a toddler's level of thinking?

Toddlers are more capable of solving problems internally, without the need for experimentation and trial and error, than younger children. Toddlers are able to think in ways that are different from the thinking of infancy because they are at the level of symbolic representation.[1] At this stage, children can mentally represent objects and events. This level of representational thought is evident through pretend play. A block becomes a car, a telephone, or a comb in the symbolic play of the older toddler.

What math knowledge emerges in toddlers?

Toddlers are able to understand "some" and "more." This understanding is apparent in both their receptive and expressive language development.

Many toddlers are able to rote count from one to five or even higher. Since language development is a major focus of this period, toddlers like to repeat the words they hear.

Toddlers vary in their understanding of quantification, but commonly understand quantities of one and two. They have a beginning understanding of one-to-one correspondence. Toddlers are aware of their hands and often want to hold one object in each hand. Shoes are an important article of clothing for toddlers, who will search until they find a pair of shoes, one for each foot!

What kinds of comments can teachers make to enhance the mathematical development of toddlers?

As children interact with materials in the classroom, teachers can make comments that include the mathematical language children will need in their future experiences with math materials, such as more, less, *and* half, *as well as the counting words.* Teachers typically make comments to describe the actions of children and the reactions of the materials. The inclusion of comments using the language of mathematics is an important component of the curriculum. These comments by the teacher stimulate interest in the materials and may encourage children to explore them in new ways.

What kinds of math questions are appropriate to use with toddlers?

The best questions for toddlers are those that focus on one-to-one correspondence and quantification of small amounts, from one to three. These types of questions are most effective when the teacher uses the child's activity as a basis for the question. For example, the teacher may ask a child in the dramatic play area if she has enough bottles for each doll to have a bottle, or how many more bottles she needs to have one bottle for each doll. These questions should be posed when the quantities are less than three.

How can teachers set up manipulative materials to encourage mathematical thinking with toddlers?

Teachers can focus on the components of manipulative materials so that the quantities and specific attributes of the manipulative pieces lead children to explore the concepts of one-to-one correspondence and quantification of small amounts. For example, when assembling a set of Duplo blocks, the teacher might include an equivalent number of people and cars. This allows toddlers to explore one-to-one correspondence as they place one person in each car. To encourage quantification of small amounts, the teacher might select six beads for stringing—two blue, two red, and two yellow. As toddlers begin to place the beads onto the string, the teacher can ask questions about the quantities of beads, such as "Do you have just as many red beads as blue beads? How many more red beads do you need to have just as many?"

Pegs, large beads for stringing, stacking toys, Duplo blocks, and other construction materials compose the bulk of the activities in the manipulative area of classrooms designed for toddlers. These materials provide many opportunities for children to explore mathematical concepts when teachers carefully plan for such outcomes. Suggestions for questions and comments to stimulate mathematical thinking are included with each activity in this chapter.

What management issues are unique for toddlers that may affect their use of math materials?

Toddlers are less able to delay gratification and may require more teacher assistance than preschool children. Teachers can provide duplicates of some activities to reduce the time toddlers spend waiting for a turn. Teachers should also consider reducing the quantity of materials in activities for toddlers, in order to eliminate a typical toddler behavior of dumping and filling containers. Cooperative activities, which include more than one child and the teacher as part of the play, are also important to include in the math curriculum for toddlers.

What special considerations should teachers make when designing math materials for toddlers?

Teachers must consider the developmental level of the group as well as the specific needs of individual children within the group. Many toddlers, even older ones, continue to explore materials by placing objects into their mouths. This poses both a safety hazard and a sanitation concern. The math activities that teachers plan for toddlers should incorporate larger objects that can be easily sanitized.

How can teachers assess math development with toddlers?

Teachers in toddler settings frequently keep daily journals or logs for parents. This is especially true for child care programs. These logs are designed to keep parents informed about eating, sleeping, and other personal care experiences of their children during the day. Information about children's math experiences can also be included. For example, the teacher may want to document instances of rote counting, one-to-one correspondence, and quantification. The teacher can copy these logs to keep on file as a way to document experiences and assess the children's progress over an extended period of time at school.

Endnotes
1. Barry J. Wadsworth, *Piaget's Theory of Cognitive and Affective Development,* 4th ed. (White Plains, NY: Longman, 1989) 51.

Math Activities
for Toddlers

4.1 Magnetic Bears and Balloons

Description

The combination of colorful teddy bears and balloons naturally attracts toddlers to this activity. The bear and balloon cutouts are laminated and have magnetic tape attached to the back. Toddlers can use the materials on a metal surface, such as a file cabinet, cookie sheet, or standard magnetic board. When teachers ask toddlers if they have enough balloons for each bear, they naturally begin to think in terms of one-to-one correspondence.

Math Concepts

▲ one-to-one correspondence
▲ quantification

Materials

▲ 5 laminated bear cutouts (the ones pictured above were made using an Elison machine)
▲ 10 laminated balloon cutouts, in 2 shapes and 2 colors
▲ self-adhesive magnetic tape

Teacher and Child Interactions

The teacher can stimulate interest in this activity in several ways. She may join a child already playing with the bears, invite a child to join her in the activity, or demonstrate the activity to a small group. The teacher may begin with two or three bears and three or four balloons, in two colors. More bears and balloons can be added as the teacher observes the level of understanding of individual children.

What to Look For

Some children will place one balloon on the paw of each bear in a one-to-one correspondence manner.

Some children will be able to approximate answers to the teacher's questions, such as whether or not there are enough balloons for each bear to have two.

Some children may play with the bears in a pretend manner.

Some children may be overwhelmed by the quantities of balloons available.

Modifications

If children have difficulty constructing one-to-one correspondence relationships between the bears and balloons, begin with one hat for each bear. The hats can be made from triangle shapes and decorated with stripes or dots.

For variety, use different colors or shapes of balloons.

Use both the hats and balloons for children who are ready to consider more complex problems to solve.

Comments and Questions to Extend Thinking

I need some balloons for my bears.

Help me give each bear a balloon.

Do we have enough balloons for each bear to have one?

Can we give each bear two balloons?

Are there enough red balloons to give one to each bear?

Integrated Curriculum Activities

Read simple books that include teddy bears, such as *Now We Can Go,* by Ann Jonas (New York: Greenwillow, 1986) and *10 Bears in My Bed,* by Stan Mack (New York: Pantheon, 1974).

Sing a short song about teddy bears that also includes the children's names (see *More Than Singing,* activity 2.1).

Teddy bear notepad pages can be used if other cutouts are not available. Balloons can be drawn freehand.

4.2 Clip the Can

Description

For this activity, a large can is painted with stripes of primary colors. Toddlers stick large, push-style clothespins onto the can, often in a one-to-one correspondence relationship with the stripes. The teacher's comments encourage children to explore the activity while she provides the appropriate math vocabulary. Several types of clips offer opportunities for toddlers to repeat the activity.

Math Concepts

▲ one-to-one correspondence
▲ quantification
▲ rote counting to six

Materials

▲ one 13-ounce can, divided into 6 sections that are painted with red, blue, and yellow nontoxic paint
▲ large wooden clothespins

Teacher and Child Interactions

Initially, many toddlers enjoy simply dropping the clothespins into the can. The teacher may redirect the activity by demonstrating how to place the clothespins onto the rim of the can. Since toddlers like turn-taking games, they typically join the teacher. The teacher may count as children place clips onto the rim of the can. This provides a model for the counting words. The teacher can also comment on how many clothespins are on each stripe, thus focusing on quantification.

What to Look For

Some children will count the clothespins with the teacher.

Some children will put one clothespin on each stripe in a one-to-one correspondence manner.

Some children may not know how to place the clothespins onto the rim of the can until the teacher models it.

Some children may place the clothespins onto the rim of the can in a random manner.

Modifications

Paint the clothespins to match the colors on the can. This encourages children to make same and different comparisons.

Use pinch-type clothespins in place of the push-type for children who are ready for a more challenging fine-motor activity.

To increase the difficulty, use a smaller can with more stripes and additional colors.

Comments and Questions to Extend Thinking

I need one clip for each stripe. Do we have enough?

One for you, one for me. This comment encourages the child to play the game with the teacher.

I need two clips. Can you give me two?

How many do we have now?

Integrated Curriculum Activities

Put several sizes of cans and a wooden beater in the music area. Children can compare the sounds of the various cans (see *More Than Magnets,* activity 6.2).

Read simple books that emphasize color, such as the board book *Brown Bear, Brown Bear, What Do You See?* by Bill Martin, Jr. (New York: Holt, 1995).

Helpful Hints

Construction paper can be used to make the colored stripes. Use clear contact paper to cover the paper and attach it to the can.

Be sure the edges of the can are not sharp.

4.3 Stinky Socks

Description

Toddlers love looking for all kinds of things. In this activity, they search for pairs of baby socks. Many parents delight their toddlers with games, such as "tickle your toes and find your nose." This activity goes with the "Stinky Socks" poem, below.

> STINKY SOCKS
> Socks in the basket, for me and you,
> Let's make a pair, here's a clue, *(hold up a sock)*
> Some of you have (green) socks too,
> Put them in the basket, if you do.
> Stinky, stinky socks—Pee-you!

Math Concepts

▲ one-to-one correspondence
▲ sorting
▲ quantification
▲ rote counting to six

Materials
▲ 4 or 5 pairs of colorful baby socks
▲ basket or box for the socks
▲ shelf extender, for hanging up the pairs of socks (optional)

Teacher and Child Interactions
Throughout the day, teachers may need to help toddlers take off and put on their socks. They can use this opportunity to compare socks that are the same and different. Teachers may wish to introduce this game to a small group and use the children's own socks. Later, pairs of brightly colored socks can be placed in the manipulative area. Children naturally begin to explore them, and some may even try to wear them! The teacher can encourage children to find pairs of matching socks. The socks can be folded together or clipped onto the shelf extender, which resembles a clothesline. Occasionally, the teacher may remove one or more of the socks, so that some pairs are incomplete. This provides an opportunity to compare sets of one and two.

What to Look For
Some children may line up the socks in a row.
Some children may place matching pairs together.
Some children may notice when the matching sock is missing.
Some children may count the socks in a pair.

Modifications
Include new pairs of socks in the activity.
Increase the quantity of pairs of socks.

Comments and Questions to Extend Thinking
Let's look for a sock like this one.
Do you have two socks that are the same?
I need one more to match this sock.
How many pairs of socks did we find?

Integrated Curriculum Activities
Put baby socks in the dramatic play area to use with dolls.
Wash socks in the water table.

Ask parents for donations of old baby socks.

4.4 Teddy Bears and Cubes

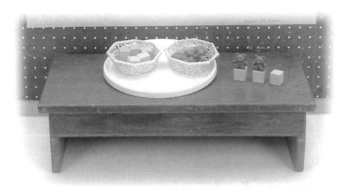

Description

Careful planning increases mathematical thinking as toddlers use familiar manipulative materials, such as large teddy bear counters and colored cubes. This game encourages toddlers to place the bears and cubes into a one-to-one correspondence relationship and to think about quantification.

Math Concepts

▲ one-to-one correspondence
▲ quantification
▲ rote counting

Materials

▲ 8 or more large teddy bear counters (2 of each color)
▲ 8 or more 1-inch cubes (include one color that is different from the bears)
▲ 2 baskets, one for the bears and one for the cubes
▲ tray, for display of the activity

Teacher and Child Interactions

Toddlers love to play stacking games and turn-taking games with the teacher. In this activity, the teacher encourages children to place the bears on top of the blocks in a one-to-one correspondence relationship. Teachers can use questioning strategies to enhance the mathematical potential in the materials. They may also model counting. The quantities of bears and cubes are small enough for children to compare.

What to Look For
Many children will place one bear on top of each cube in a one-to-one correspondence relationship.

Some children will count the bears after they have heard this modeled.

Initially, children may stack the cubes on top of each other and not think about a one-to-one relationship between the bears and the cubes.

Some children may play with the bears in a pretend way.

Modification
Use more teddy bears and cubes.

Questions to Extend Thinking
Do you have enough bears to sit on each block?

How many more bears do you need for your cubes?

Are there as many red bears as green bears?

Integrated Curriculum Activities
Use teddy bear cookie cutters with playdough.

Let children act out the familiar children's rhyme, "Teddy Bear, Teddy Bear, Turn Around."

Helpful Hints
The small teddy bear counters are unacceptable, since they are a choking hazard.

4.5 First Grid Game

Description
This is a good beginning grid game for older toddlers and young preschool children. The game boards have only six spaces with silhouette stickers of children. The cover-up pieces are plastic hats. Children seem to naturally want to give each silhouette a hat.

Math Concepts
▲ one-to-one correspondence
▲ quantification
▲ creation and comparison of sets

Materials
▲ 2 black grid boards (5 by 11 inches) marked into 6 spaces
▲ 12 silhouette stickers of children
▲ 12 plastic hats (large enough to not pose a choking hazard)
▲ spinner, divided into sections with 1, 2, or 3 dots per section (optional)

Teacher and Child Interactions
Toddlers often match objects by color, such as looking for a hat in the same color as the sticker. When the teacher joins the activity and observes this, he can focus attention on mathematical concepts through specific questioning strategies.

What to Look For
Some children will attempt to place the hats onto the stickers in a one-to-one correspondence manner.
A few children may count the hats they have.
Some children will place all the hats in a row across the grid without regard for one-to-one correspondence.
Many children will play with the hats or match by color.

Modifications

Use large teddy bear counters from activity 4.4 in place of the hats.
Include the optional spinner as part of the activity. Children may
begin to quantify according to the dots on the spinner.

Comments and Questions to Extend Thinking

Do you have one hat for each child?
I have a red hat for this person. (Place the hat on a sticker of a
different color to direct attention away from color matching.)
How many more hats do you need for the children?

Integrated Curriculum Activity

Put hats in the dramatic play area for dress-up (activity 1.3).

Helpful Hints

Be sure to use some
hats that are different in
color from the stickers
to encourage children to
think about concepts
other than color
matching.

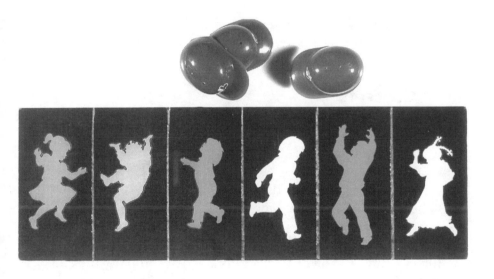

4.6 Rings and Ducks

Description

Brightly colored rings invite toddlers to place one rubber duck into each ring, which makes this a good one-to-one correspondence activity. Teachers may wish to sing a variation of the song "Five Little Ducks," as children use this activity. Begin the song with "Three little ducks went out to play."

Math Concepts

▲ one-to-one correspondence
▲ creation and comparison of sets

Materials

▲ 3 small rubber or plastic ducks
▲ 3 plastic rings, slightly larger than the ducks

Teacher and Child Interactions

Toddlers enjoy singing or hearing songs to accompany their play. Teachers may engage the children in this activity by singing "Three Little Ducks," which encourages children to place the ducks inside the rings. Teachers can ask questions to focus attention on one-to-one correspondence and the comparison of sets.

What to Look For

Children often respond to the questions or comments of the teacher and attempt to place one duck into each ring.

Some children may compare sets of ducks in the rings and sets of ducks not in a ring.

Many children will play with the ducks by pretending to have them swim or talk to each other.

Modifications

For variety, use small rubber frogs in place of the ducks.

For children who are ready to deal with larger amounts, increase the quantity of ducks included in the activity.

Comments and Questions to Extend Thinking

Do you have enough rings for each duck to play in a ring?

How many more ducks still need a ring?

Two little ducks went out to play. How many are still left? (Make this comment and ask this question if you sing the song as children play with the ducks and rings.)

Integrated Curriculum Activities

Put rubber ducks in the water table.

Add a book version of the song "Five Little Ducks" to the reading area. Teachers can make their own book with duck stickers.

The rings can be made using ¼-inch plastic tubing from a hardware store.

4.7 Cars and People

Description

Duplo blocks and accessories are a common component of toddler programs. The pieces are large, fairly easy to assemble, and provide opportunities for toddlers to engage in pretend play. They may build houses with the blocks and then drive the Duplo cars to the houses. This activity provides teachers with the opportunity to ask questions that encourage the development of quantification strategies with small quantities of objects.

Math Concepts
▲ one-to-one correspondence
▲ quantification
▲ creation and comparison of sets

Materials
▲ basket of Duplo blocks
▲ 3 Duplo cars
▲ 3 Duplo people

Teacher and Child Interactions

As toddlers explore manipulative materials such as Duplo blocks, teachers often interact with them by commenting on the colors or sizes of the blocks. Teachers can also make comments related to mathematical concepts, such as one-to-one correspondence and comparison of sets. In order to take advantage of teachable moments that might arise, teachers should select quantities of cars and people congruent with toddler levels of mathematical understanding.

What to Look For

Some children will put one person in each car in a one-to-one correspondence relationship.

Some children will compare the quantities of cars and people.

Some children will count the people and cars, particularly if they have heard this modeled.

Many children will initially build with the blocks and play with the cars and people.

Some children may ignore the teacher's questions and continue to use the materials in a construction manner.

Modification

Include additional Duplo people. This provides opportunities for questions related to quantities of two or more, such as "Do you have enough people to put two in each car?"

Questions to Extend Thinking

Do you have enough cars so that each person can ride in a car?

How many more cars do you need to have one car for each person?

How many more people do you need to have two people in each car?

Integrated Curriculum Activities

Put plastic cars in the block area.

Sing familiar songs related to vehicles, such as "The Wheels on the Bus."

Text from the song "Soft White Snowflakes" by Sally Moomaw © 1996 (see More Than Singing, *activity 6.6).*

4.8 Build a Snowman

Description

Many toddlers experience the first snowfall they actually remember during their second year. They are usually fascinated by building a snowman. For this activity, toddlers build snowmen on wooden dowels using large macramé beads that are painted white to look like snowballs. This encourages them to think about quantification to three.

Math Concepts

▲ one-to-one correspondence
▲ creation and comparison of sets
▲ quantification

Materials

▲ 1 or more dowel frames, made by drilling 7/16-inch holes in a wooden base and gluing 5-inch lengths of 7/16-inch diameter dowels into the holes
▲ 6 or more 1½-inch diameter macramé beads with ½-inch holes, painted white
▲ a 1–3 teacher-made die, made by adhering ¼-inch round file folder stickers to a 1-inch cube in sets of from 1 to 3

Teacher and Child Interactions

This activity is placed in the manipulative area for children to explore. As the teacher interacts with children, she can make comments about the snowmen the children build, model the use of the die, and ask appropriate questions to stimulate mathematical thinking.

What to Look For

Some children may roll the die, point to one dot, and place one bead onto the dowel.

Some children may place one bead on the dowel regardless of the quantity of dots on the die.

Some children will place the large beads onto the dowels without regard for the die.

Children will talk about snowmen they make.

Some children will respond to the quantification questions the teacher poses.

Modification

Include a plastic or felt hat for the top of the snowmen.

Questions to Extend Thinking

How many beads do you need for each snowman?

How many more beads do you need to finish this snowman?

Are each of the snowmen made with the same number of beads?

Integrated Curriculum Activities

Introduce the board book version of *The Snowman,* by Raymond Briggs (Boston: Little, Brown, 1985).

Sing simple snow songs (see *More Than Singing,* activities 2.6, 4.5, and 6.6).

Recite the "5 Little Snowmen" poem (activity 5.5), but reduce the number of snowmen to two and use two fingers for a finger play.

Helpful Hints

Spray paint is a quick and easy way to color several beads at one time. Use nontoxic paint.

Be sure the beads are large enough not to pose a choking hazard.

4.9 One in the Bed

Description

The song and book "Ten in the Bed" are familiar to many teachers of preschool children. Teachers recognize that counting backwards from ten is too difficult for toddlers. This activity is a variation of the "Ten in the Bed" song. Children place small people onto a doll bed as they sing a modification of the original song. The song begins with one and adds one person for each verse of the song.

There was one in the bed,
And the little one said,
"I'm lonely. I'm lonely."

So another climbed in,
And then there were two . . .

Math Concepts
▲ one-to-one correspondence
▲ quantification
▲ rote counting to three, four, or five

Materials
▲ small wooden dollhouse bed
▲ 3 to 5 small people, such as Duplo or Fisher-Price people

Teacher and Child Interactions

Teachers may wish to introduce the song at group time and use the materials as they sing the song. Later, the activity can be placed in a basket near the book area or in the manipulative area. When teachers observe children exploring the materials, they can begin to sing the song. This encourages children to think about how many people they have and how many they need. They also may compare how many are in the bed and how many still have to go to bed.

What to Look For

Some children will attend to the teacher as she sings the song and add a person for each verse.

Some children may quantify how many people are in the bed at the beginning and end of each verse.

Some children will place all the people in the bed at once.

Modifications

For children who are ready, add more people to provide opportunities for children to quantify larger amounts.

Sing the traditional version of the song, but start with three people in the bed instead of ten. Remove one person with each verse.

Comments and Questions to Extend Thinking

How many people are in the bed now?

How many more people will you put in the bed?

One, two, three. There are three in the bed.

If one more person gets into bed, how many will there be?

Integrated Curriculum Activities

Read a book version of the "Ten in the Bed" song, such as *There Were Ten in the Bed,* by Pam Adams (Singapore: Child's Play, 1979).

Sing "Three in the Bed" as children play with dolls in the dramatic play area. They may choose to put one doll in the doll bed for each verse of the song.

A bed can be made using a small cardboard shoe box. Glue fabric or wallpaper to it for decoration.

4.10 Shut the Drawer

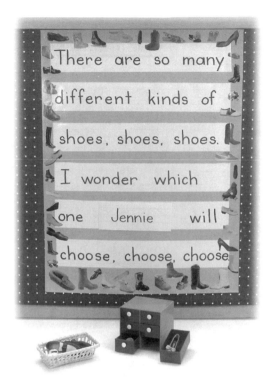

Poem by Nancy Struewing.

Description

A small plastic box and doll shoes provide a high-interest activity for toddlers, who like to open drawers to find the surprise inside. This game encourages one-to-one correspondence and beginning quantification concepts as children place one shoe inside each drawer.

Math Concepts

▲ one-to-one correspondence
▲ quantification
▲ rote counting to six

Materials

▲ 1 colorful plastic box with 6 drawers
▲ variety of small shoes (large enough not to be a choking hazard)

Teacher and Child Interactions

This activity is placed in the manipulative area for children to explore. They enjoy experimenting with opening and closing the drawers. Teachers may join the activity and pose questions to stimulate mathematical thinking, such as focusing children's attention on one shoe for each drawer or quantifying the total number of shoes.

What to Look For

Some children may place one shoe in each drawer.
Some children may attempt to place more than one shoe in each
  drawer.
Some children may attempt to quantify the total of all the shoes.

Modifications

Other small, intriguing items can be substituted for the shoes.
For an easier version of the activity, use a box with fewer drawers.

Comments and Questions to Extend Thinking

Do you have one shoe for each drawer?
How many more drawers need a shoe?
I have two shoes. Do you have a drawer for each one?

Integrated Curriculum Activities

Paint the bottom of children's feet and let them make footprints on
  a roll of shelf paper.
Use the doll shoes with playdough. Children can make impressions
  in the playdough with the shoes.

Small boxes with drawers are often found in craft and hardware stores.

More Math Manipulatives

Willy eagerly played an elephant stacking game with his teacher. Each time he rolled the dice, he counted the dots and then stacked an equivalent number of small blocks on the back of a plastic elephant. As the stack grew higher and higher, a crowd of spectators collected around the math table. Whenever the teacher or Willy rolled the dice, the watchful children squealed with delight as they too computed how many more blocks the players must attempt to balance on the elephant's back. The stack of blocks began to sway and teeter. Suddenly, as Willy placed one more block on the elephant's back, the entire tower crashed onto the table. Willy and all of his friends roared with laughter. Then everyone began to collect the blocks and return them to their basket so that another game could begin.

▲ ▲ ▲

Math manipulatives give children the opportunity to repeatedly think about math concepts as they respond to the play challenges posed by the materials. Frequently, other children are drawn to the excitement of the games, and collective negotiation and problem solving emerge. Children are challenged to broaden their thinking as they listen to the ideas of their peers and discuss the ramifications of each roll of the dice or spin of the spinner.

Teachers' Questions
What are math manipulatives?

Math manipulatives are games or activities that combine intriguing counters or manipulative pieces with the challenge of creating mathematical sets. In some manipulative games, children roll a die, spin a spinner, or select a playing card to determine the quantity of counters they must take. Other math manipulative materials combine quantification with interactive charts or counting books.

Why are math manipulatives important?

Math manipulatives allow children to create sets with movable objects. They also encourage children to quantify and to compare sets. When playing with math manipulatives, children can handle the counters or manipulative pieces as they attempt to assemble the amount required for each turn of the game. This allows each child to use a mathematical strategy commensurate with his or her level of thinking. For example, children at a global stage of quantification can take many counters or just a few, depending on the quantity the die, spinner, or game card selected appears to indicate. Children at the one-to-one correspondence level can align counters with the dots on the die, spinner, or card, and children at the counting stage can count the required number of manipulative pieces. Children must constantly compare sets as they attempt to assemble the necessary number of counters to correspond with the quantity indicated by the game. They also frequently compare amounts with one another as they monitor the progress of the game.

What concepts emerge as children use math manipulatives?

Children construct equivalent sets, discover one-to-one correspondence relationships, and begin to explore addition and subtraction concepts as they interact with math manipulatives. As children attempt to decide how many manipulative pieces to put on a chart or how many counters to take in a game, they must constantly create and compare sets. They form one-to-one correspondence relationships as they learn to carefully align one counter with each dot on a die or say one counting word each time they take a manipulative piece. Gradually, children become interested in accumulating totals as they add game pieces to their collections. They may also begin to roll two dice and discover that they can count all the dots together to find the total. Thus, concepts of addition begin to emerge. As children try to figure out how many more pieces they need to reach a designated amount, they begin to think about subtraction. Games that encourage children to take away counters (activity 5.11) also foster the emergence of subtraction concepts.

What guides teachers in choosing or creating math manipulative materials?

Teachers often select or design math manipulatives to build upon children's interests or to coordinate with other curriculum materials in the classroom. Teachers constantly evaluate children's levels of mathematical reasoning and select math manipulatives to reinforce or extend children's thinking. Good math manipulatives are highly motivating to young children because the game format is exciting and the movable pieces are intriguing. When the manipulative material relates to a topic of special interest to a group of children, it is even more motivating. Teachers often find that coordinating math activities with other curriculum materials in the classroom heightens children's interest in all of the materials. For example, children immediately want to play a math game that corresponds with a favorite book. They may then wish to reread the book. Suggestions for integrated curriculum materials are included with each activity.

What are some unusual math manipulatives?

Math manipulatives that incorporate physical-knowledge experiences, such as stacking and balancing, offer new challenges for children who are accustomed to the more typical die and counter math games. Activities such as the "Elephant Stacking Game" (activity 5.1), "Twin Towers" (activity 5.2), and "Teeter-Totter Tips" (activity 5.9) all integrate both physical-knowledge experimentation and mathematical reasoning in a game format. The physical-knowledge component adds an element of excitement to math games.

Math manipulatives that utilize materials not usually found in the classroom are also highly intriguing to young children. For example, the downspout used in "Itsy Bitsy Spiders" (activity 5.3) immediately draws children's attention. While they may have noticed downspouts on houses, they have typically not had the opportunity to handle one. Thus, adding spider magnets to the downspout as a math activity may be more interesting for some children than just collecting toy spiders.

Coordinating math activities with favorite songs or interactive charts increases their appeal for some children. Children who are more comfortable with books or language activities may readily gravitate towards a math manipulative that involves a book, song, or chart. "Crunchy Cookies" (activity 5.6) is one example.

What are the easiest math manipulatives?

The easiest math manipulatives incorporate a large die or spinner with relatively large counters that are easy for young children to handle. Quantities on the die or spinner are limited to three. Extensive observations of children in our classrooms indicate that young children can first process quantities of one to three items. Anything beyond that is viewed as "a lot." Teacher-made dice and spinners can limit amounts to correspond to the mathematical reasoning levels of young children. Quarter-inch round file stickers mounted on one-inch cubes make excellent dice for young children.

What types of math manipulatives are more challenging for older or more advanced children?

Math activities that utilize two or more dice and larger quantities of counters or manipulative pieces are more complex. Using two dice introduces children to the concept of adding two sets of numbers. At first, many children count the two dice separately before selecting their counters, and they do not understand that they could get the same total by counting all of the dots together. Once children arrive at this realization, they need many opportunities to experience the results of adding two sets. Counting errors are common. Eventually, children solidify their counting skills and begin to remember addition combinations. At this point, some children may wish to add a third or fourth die to their games to further increase the complexity. Special dice, such as ten-sided or spherical dice, also add interest for more experienced children.

How should teachers guide children in their use of math manipulatives?

Teachers should encourage children to use their own thinking strategies to solve math problems. Telling children how to get the correct answer, such as moving the child's finger while counting, does not help children learn to think logically. Instead, it imposes the adult's thinking on the child and teaches children to look to adults to solve math problems. Children need many opportunities to think about mathematical relationships in order to develop their sense of number.

Teachers can encourage children to discuss mathematical problems that emerge as they interact and play games together. Discussion and disagreement among peers do not inhibit children's autonomy and willingness to think about solutions to problems. Often, as children try to explain a viewpoint to another child, new ways of thinking emerge. Children learn from one another because they think and evaluate as they argue and discuss.

Teachers can subtly guide children by modeling mathematical reasoning at a stage that is just above the thinking level of the child. Thus, if a child is at a global level of quantification, the teacher might model one-to-one correspondence; if a child is at a one-to-one correspondence level, the teacher might model counting. Modeling is not the same as correcting errors. It simply offers an alternative means to solve a problem.

What if the teacher is involved with other issues in the classroom and is often not available to play math games with children?

The potential for mathematical learning is imbedded in the materials and in the interactions among peers as they play with math manipulatives. Dice and spinners naturally encourage children to quantify and to create and compare sets. Due to the game nature of many of the materials, children frequently play them with a friend. As children discuss the progress of the game, they fuel each other's thinking. Data collected in our classrooms over a period of many years strongly affirms that children make substantial progress in their mathematical thinking even when the teacher is not a prominent part of their interactions with math manipulatives and games. This observation is not meant to discourage teachers from interacting with children in the math area, as teacher modeling and questioning strategies can be very valuable. However, it may serve to reassure teachers that learning occurs even when they are not directly involved.

How can teachers assess children's mathematical thinking through their use of math manipulatives?

Teachers can carefully observe children to determine what mathematical concepts they are exploring and their level of mathematical reasoning when quantifying. Over time, teachers can watch for a progression in each child's thinking. When interacting with children, teachers may ask leading questions to explore children's reasoning and problem-solving strategies. Each activity in this book offers suggestions for questions that teachers may use to extend children's thinking. Teachers may wish to record their observations anecdotally or use the assessment form in the appendix.

More Math Manipulative Activities

5.1 Elephant Stacking Game

Description

This is an exciting manipulative game for children of many ages. Children take turns rolling dice and attempting to stack an equivalent number of small blocks or disks on the back of a toy elephant. Each player tries not to be the one to topple the stack. The game combines the physical-knowledge challenge of balancing the tallest stack of blocks possible with the math concepts of creating and comparing sets.

Math Concepts
▲ quantification
▲ creation and comparison of sets
▲ addition

Materials
▲ Duplo elephant, or other toy animal with a flat back
▲ small blocks (¼-inch-thick plastic blocks, called Rainbow Counters, were used in the photo)
▲ 1 or 2 dice

Child's Level
This activity is appropriate for both preschool and kindergarten children.

What to Look For

Children will try to create the highest possible tower of blocks.

Children will quantify the amount on the die and try to add an equivalent number of blocks to the stack.

Some children will stack blocks without regard to the number shown on the die.

Children will discover that a large number can be a hindrance because it increases their odds of knocking over the tower.

Some children will roll two dice and add the sets together to get the total.

Modifications

For younger children, use a 1–3 die and 1-inch cubes for stacking. You can make the die by applying ¼-inch round file stickers to a 1-inch cube. One-inch cubes may be easier for young children to manipulate than thinner blocks.

For older children who can handle larger quantities, use two dice and poker chips for stacking. Since poker chips are thin, many more can be piled on the elephant's back before they fall.

Questions to Extend Thinking

How can you tell how many blocks to put on the elephant's back?

Do you think Katrina can balance six more blocks on the elephant's back?

Should I hope for a big number or a little number when I roll the dice?

How many blocks do you think we can balance on our tower?

Integrated Curriculum Activities

Include zoo animals in the block or manipulative areas.

Provide other types of materials for stacking.

Read books about zoo animals, such as *Dear Zoo,* by Rod Campbell (Washington, DC: Four Winds, 1982).

Helpful Hints

Put a square Duplo block on the back of the elephant before stacking the blocks. This creates a flat surface to support the block tower.

5.2 Twin Towers

Description
In this construction game, children take turns rolling one or two dice and adding an equivalent number of construction pieces to their tower. Players try to build the tallest building possible without knocking it over.

Math Concepts
▲ creation and comparison of sets
▲ quantification
▲ addition

Materials
▲ construction manipulative material, such as Rig-a-ma-jigs, Duplo blocks, table blocks
▲ 1 or 2 dice

Child's Level
This activity is appropriate for both preschool and kindergarten children.

What to Look For

Some children will roll the dice to decide how many pieces to add to their buildings.

Children will compare the height of their towers.

Children will select a quantification strategy (global, one-to-one correspondence, or counting) commensurate with their level of thinking.

Some children will add two dice together by counting all the dots.

Modification

Switch to a teacher-made 1–3 die if a standard die is too difficult. Quarter-inch round file stickers mounted on a 1-inch cube work well.

Questions to Extend Thinking

How many pieces will you add to your tower?

If you roll a three, will your tower be higher than Angki's?

How many does Sijia need to have a tower as tall as yours?

How many more blocks do you think you can add to your tower before it falls over?

Integrated Curriculum Activities

Set up a construction site in the dramatic play area.

Read books about skyscrapers, such as *Skyscraper Going Up,* by Vicki Cobb (New York: Crowell, 1987).

Plan a gross-motor construction game. Children can roll a giant die and carry a cardboard block as they hop along a path to the construction site.

Helpful Hints

Provide a large tray for the children to stack their blocks on. This will help contain the blocks when they crash.

5.3 Itsy-Bitsy Spiders

Description

For this game, children spin a spider spinner to determine how many magnetized plastic spiders to place on their metal downspout. Children can quantify how many spiders they have at the end of the game and compare the results.

Math Concepts

▲ quantification
▲ creation and comparison of sets
▲ addition

Materials

▲ 1 or 2 metal downspout sections, each with a 90-degree elbow joint
▲ plastic spiders, with pieces of magnetic tape glued to them
▲ spider spinner, made by adhering spider stickers or confetti to a blank spinner in sets of 1 to 4

Child's Level

This game is appropriate for both preschool and kindergarten children. Older or more experienced children may choose to play the game like a path game, as suggested in the modification.

What to Look For

Some children will spin the spinner to determine how many spiders to put on their downspout.

Some children will compare how many spiders they each have.

Some children will initially stick spiders to the spouts without regard to the quantity. They may be more interested in the magnetic properties of the spiders than in how many they have. Later, they may begin to quantify the spiders.

Modification

For more advanced children, create a path on the downspouts with horizontal strips of plastic tape. Children can move the spiders up the spouts as in a short path game (see chapter 7).

Questions to Extend Thinking

Do you have as many spiders as Lucy?

How many spiders will you have if you get two more?

If one spider falls off the spout, how many will you have left?

How can we find out which spout has the most spiders?

Integrated Curriculum Activities

Sing the "Itsy-Bitsy Spider" as children play the game.

Read books about spiders and insects.

Put a large model of a spider and an insect in the science area so children can compare them.

Take a nature walk and look for spider webs. Spray the webs with water to make them more visible.

Downspout pieces can be purchased from hardware or building supply stores. They can be taped to a room divider or the back of a shelf to hold them in place.

Use a hot glue gun to mount the magnetic tape to the spiders.

5.4 Spider Webs

Thanks to Dena Papin for this idea.

Description
Each child has a plastic spider web in this manipulative game. Children take turns drawing cards to determine how many spiders or insects to place on their webs.

Math Concepts
▲ quantification
▲ creation and comparison of sets
▲ addition

Materials
▲ 2 plastic spider webs
▲ small plastic spiders or insects
▲ spider cards, made by affixing sets of 1 to 6 spider stickers on orange index cards

Child's Level
This activity is appropriate for both preschool and kindergarten children.

What to Look For
Some children will requantify the number of spiders on the cards and attempt to take an equivalent number of spiders for their webs.

Children will select a quantification strategy (global, one-to-one correspondence, or counting) commensurate with their level of thinking.

Some children will compare the amount of spiders on each other's webs.

Some children will requantify the total number of spiders they have each time they add more.

Modifications

For younger children, limit the number of spiders on the cards to three.

Older children can draw two cards and add the quantities.

Questions to Extend Thinking

How can you tell how many spiders to take?

Which web do you think has more spiders?

How many spiders will you have if you add one more spider?

Integrated Curriculum Activities

Read or sing spider song books such as *Spider on the Floor,* by Raffi (New York: Crown, 1993) and *The Itsy Bitsy Spider,* by Iza Trapani (Boston: Whispering Coyote, 1993).

Add plastic spiders and insects to sand in the sensory table. Children can use slotted spoons to pick up the bugs.

Put a collection of plastic spiders and insects in the manipulative area for sorting and classifying.

Helpful Hints

Look for plastic spiders and webs in party supply stores, especially before Halloween.

Remind children that most spider webs only have one spider.

5.5   5 Little Snowmen

Description

This activity encourages children to think about subtraction. It combines a snowman poem, set in big book format, with snowmen cutouts to add to the book pages. Each time children complete a verse of the poem, they must subtract one snowman from the total. Blank pockets made from clear laminating film or acetate provide a space for children to place the necessary number of snowmen.

5 Little Snowmen

Brenda Hieronymus
© 1986

5 little snowmen standing in a row,
1, 2, 3, 4, 5 they go,
Out came the sun and it shone all day,
1 little snowman melted away.

4 little snowmen standing in a row,
1, *, 2, 3, 4 they go,
Out came the sun and it shone all day,
1 little snowman melted away.

3 little snowmen standing in a row,
1, *, 2, *, 3 they go,
Out came the sun and it shone all day,
1 little snowman melted away.

2 little snowmen standing in a row,
1, *, *, *, 2 they go,
Out came the sun and it shone all day,
1 little snowman melted away.

1 little snowman standing all alone,
But the sun no longer shone,
Out came the children and they built 4,
5 little snowmen together once more.

*(Note: * denotes a silence.)*

Math Concepts

▲ quantification
▲ subtraction
▲ addition

Materials

▲ 6 pieces of blue construction paper (18 by 24 inches)
▲ white sentence strips
▲ clear acetate or laminating film
▲ 20 snowmen cutouts

Directions

Carefully print each line of the poem on a sentence strip, with one verse of the poem allotted for each sheet of paper. Allow a space between lines 2 and 3 for a pocket made from acetate or extra laminating film. Laminate the pages before adding the pocket. Children can add laminated snowmen cutouts to the pocket or take them away, as indicated by the words.

Child's Level

This activity is appropriate for both preschool and kindergarten children.

What to Look For

Children will attempt to place the same number of snowmen in the pocket as indicated in each verse.

Children may have disagreements about how many snowmen are in the pocket.

Some children will subtract one snowman each time one melts in the poem.

Modification

Older children may want to write their own version of the poem with more snowmen.

Questions to Extend Thinking

How many snowmen should go into the pocket?
How many snowmen are left now that one melted?
If two snowmen melt, will there be any left?

Integrated Curriculum Activities

Add colored ice cubes to water in the sensory table. Children can watch the colors mix as the ice melts. To make the colored ice, add food coloring to water in the ice trays before freezing.

Paint with ice cubes. Freeze water colored with food coloring in ice cube trays that have small compartments. Children can draw with the colored ice.

Helpful Hints

The pocket can be taped to the pages with clear packing tape.

5.6 Crunchy Cookies

Description
This activity combines a counting song with an interactive chart. It encourages children to construct equivalent sets as they add cookies to the chart. The manipulative pieces (cookies) allow children to visualize the sets they are creating.

Math Concepts
▲ quantification
▲ creation and comparison of sets
▲ addition

Crunchy Cookies

1 crunch-y cook- ie, 2 crunch-y cook- ies, 3 crunch-y cook- ies,

4. We'll roll and roll and shape and bake and then make man- y more.

© Copyright, Brenda Hieronymus

Materials
▲ brown poster board (22 by 28 inches)
▲ sentence strips
▲ picture, to illustrate the song
▲ cookie magnets (more than 4, so that children have to think about how many to place on the chart)
▲ strip of magnetic tape at the top of the chart to hold the cookies

Child's Level
This activity is appropriate for both preschool and kindergarten children.

What to Look For

Children will add cookies to the chart to match the number in
each line of the song.

Children will discuss how many cookies are on the chart.

Some children will recount all of the cookies each time one is
added to the chart.

Some children will add one to the total, without having to re-count
all the cookies, each time one is added to the chart.

Modification

For older or more advanced children, include movable numeral
cards with larger numbers to mount on the chart in the places
where numbers are used, and provide more cookie magnets. Children can choose which numbers to sing in the song and add the
appropriate amount of cookies to the chart.

Questions to Extend Thinking

Can you show what one crunchy cookie would look like on
the chart?

How many cookies do we have to add to have two crunchy
cookies?

If we ate two cookies, how many would be left?

Integrated Curriculum Activities

Set up a bakery in the dramatic play area. Include gridded cookie
sheets and magnetic cookies to encourage mathematical thinking (activity 1.1).

Include *The Doorbell Rang*, by Pat Hutchins (New York: Greenwillow, 1986) in the book area, and read the big book version at
group time.

Bake cookies with the children.

Helpful Hints

Laminate the chart
before adding the strip
of magnetic tape.

Be sure the strip of
magnetic tape is long
enough to hold more
than four cookies. This
will encourage children
to think about the num-
ber of cookies on the
board rather than just
filling all of the available
space.

5.7 Pots and Flowers

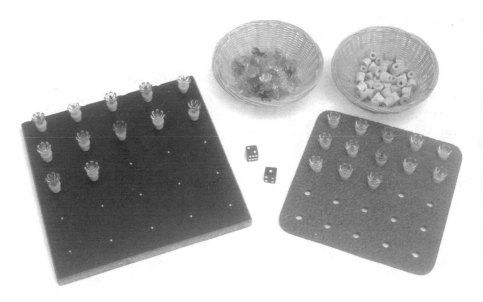

Thanks to Nancy Struewing for this idea.

Description

In this manipulative game, children roll dice and fill small wooden flowerpots with plastic flowers. The flowers are Christmas tree light holders. The wooden flowerpots fit into holes in a large foam pegboard or over the nails on a geoboard. They can also be glued to a wooden base plate if desired. Since only one flower fits in each pot, children are encouraged to put the flowers and pots into a one-to-one correspondence relationship. Children can roll the die or dice to determine how many pots to take, and then they can roll again for the flowers.

Math Concepts

▲ one-to-one correspondence
▲ quantification
▲ creation and comparison of sets
▲ addition
▲ subtraction

Materials

▲ 40 small wooden flowerpots (½ inch in diameter)
▲ 40 flower-shaped Christmas tree light holders
▲ 2 large-hole pegboards or 2 geoboards (optional)
▲ 2 wooden base plates (optional)
▲ 1 or 2 dice

Child's Level

This activity is most appropriate for older preschool or kinder-garten children, who can more easily manipulate the small pots and flowers.

What to Look For

Some children will put one flower in each pot without regard to the dice. They are working on one-to-one correspondence rela-tionships.

Some children will roll the dice to determine how many pots and flowers to take.

Some children will compare how many pots they have with how many flowers they have.

Some children will quantify how many pots and flowers they have at the end of the game.

Children will select a quantification strategy (global, one-to-one correspondence, or counting) commensurate with their level of thinking.

Modifications

For younger or less experienced children, start with a 1–3 die.

For more advanced children, add a second die and additional pots and flowers.

Comments and Questions to Extend Thinking

Do you have enough flowers for each pot?

How do you know how many pots to take?

How many more flowers do you have than pots?

I get to take two more pots. I wonder how many I have now.

Integrated Curriculum Activities

Plant flowers with the children.

Read books about flowers, such as *Flower Garden,* by Eve Bunting (New York: Harcourt, 1994).

Include dried flower petals as collage materials in the art area. (Ask a local florist to save them for your class.)

Display cut flowers in the classroom, both for their aesthetic appeal and to encourage young artists.

Set up a flower shop in the dramatic play area.

Look for the wooden flowerpots in craft stores or novelty catalogs.

The flowerpots can be painted with terra-cotta acrylic paint to make them look even more like real flowerpots.

5.8 Ice-Cream Treats

Description

For this game, children create ice-cream cones by placing wooden cones and macramé beads in ice-cream colors on a dowel frame. Each child can construct four ice-cream cones. There are even cherries to put on the top. A roll of the dice tells the players how many scoops to add to the cones.

Math Concepts

▲ creation and comparison of sets
▲ quantification
▲ addition
▲ multiplication

Materials

▲ 2 dowel frames, made by drilling four ¼-inch holes in a wooden base (12 by 2 inches) and gluing 9-inch lengths of ¼-inch diameter dowels into the holes
▲ assortment of large-hole macramé beads, painted ice-cream flavor colors with acrylic paint
▲ plastic cherries for the top of the cone, with a ¼-inch hole drilled in the bottom (red macramé beads can be substituted)
▲ small clay or wooden flowerpots (1-inch diameter) to use for the cones
▲ a 1–6 die

Child's Level

This activity is most appropriate for older preschool or kindergarten children.

What to Look For

Children will stack the beads on the dowels to create ice-cream
cones.

Some children will quantify the number of scoops of ice cream on
each cone.

Some children will compare how many of each flavor they have.

Some children will put the same number of scoops on each dowel
and then quantify them (multiplication).

Children will try to fill up each cone.

Some children will create patterns with the beads.

Some children will sort the beads by color.

Modifications

Switch to a 1–3 die for younger children.

For more advanced children, use longer dowels and more
macramé beads. Kindergarten children may wish to graph the
quantities of each flavor that they have on their cones.

Questions to Extend Thinking

How many scoops did it take to fill up your cone?

Do you have more chocolate or strawberry?

If you fill up two cones, how many scoops will you have?
(multiplication)

How many cherries do you need to have one for each
ice-cream cone?

If you don't put a cherry on top, how many scoops can fit?

Integrated Curriculum Activities

Transform the dramatic play area into an ice-cream parlor
(activity 1.15).

Make an interactive chart out of the poem "Bleezer's Ice Cream"
from *The New Kid on the Block,* by Jack Prelutsky (New York:
Greenwillow, 1984). Children can make up their own outlandish
flavors to add to the chart.

Sing ice-cream songs (see *More Than Singing,* activity 4.2).

Take a field trip to an ice-cream parlor.

Make ice cream with the children (see *More Than Magnets,*
activity 7.6).

Helpful Hints

If you are using wooden
flowerpots for cones,
drill holes in the bot-
toms if they don't
already have them.

If you are using flower-
pots for cones, be sure
to select a dowel size
that fits through the
hole in the pot.

5.9　Teeter-Totter Tips

Description
This game combines physical-knowledge discoveries with math. Children roll a die to determine how many teddy bear counters to place on their side of the teeter-totter. They can observe the effect on the seesaw as teddy bears are added. Children can determine whether the up or down side wins, or work together to try to balance the teeter-totter for the end of the game.

Math Concepts
▲ creation and comparison of sets
▲ quantification
▲ addition

Materials
▲ teeter-totter from a manipulative toy
▲ teddy bear counters
▲ teddy bear die, made by adhering small teddy bear stickers to a 1-inch cube in sets of 1 to 4

Child's Level
This activity is appropriate for both preschool and kindergarten children.

What to Look For

Children will roll the die to determine how many teddy bears to place on their side of the teeter-totter.

Children will notice the effect on the teeter-totter as more teddy bears are added.

Some children will compare the quantities of teddy bears on each side of the teeter-totter.

Some children will attempt to balance the teeter-totter.

Some children will discover that the position of the teddy bears on the teeter-totter, as well as the quantity, affects the balance.

Modification

For children who are ready to work with larger quantities, switch to a type of counter that can be stacked, such as poker chips, and use one or two regular dice.

Questions to Extend Thinking

How many teddy bears do you have on your side of the teeter-totter?

What do you think will happen when you add three more?

Why is this side of the teeter-totter lower?

How many more bears do you think you need to balance the teeter-totter?

Integrated Curriculum Activities

Add a teeter-totter to the gross-motor area. (See *More Than Magnets,* activity 8.9, for a unique adaptation.)

Put a balance scale in the science area. (See *More Than Magnets,* activity 3.9, for ideas.)

Helpful Hints

If children have trouble remembering which side of the teeter-totter is theirs, color code the two sides with strips of plastic tape or colored contact paper.

5.10 Birds on a Wire

Description

Children often observe birds sitting on telephone wires. For this game, each child has a telephone pole and wire frame made from wooden dowels and wrapped wire. They also have small birds to clip onto the wires. A spinner or die determines how many birds each child can add to the wire with each turn.

Math Concepts

▲ creation and comparison of sets
▲ quantification
▲ addition

Materials

▲ telephone pole frame (see directions below)
▲ small wooden or flocked birds, secured to small pinch clothes-pins with a hot glue gun
▲ bird spinner, made by adhering sets of 1 to 4 bird stickers to a blank spinner

Directions

To make the telephone pole frame, cut two 8-inch lengths of ¾-inch-diameter dowel. Drill a ¼-inch hole through each dowel near the top. Insert and glue a 5-inch length of ¼-inch dowel in each hole. Drill a ¾-inch-diameter hole at either end of a wood base (15 by 4 inches). Glue the ¾-inch-diameter dowels into the holes. Stretch plastic-wrapped wire between the crossbars of the telephone poles.

Child's Level

This game is most appropriate for older preschool or kindergarten children, who can more easily manipulate the birds.

What to Look For
Children will spin the spinner to determine how many birds to put
  on their wire.
At first, some children may clip birds to the wire without regard to
  the spinner. They are exploring the physical properties of the
  clips and balancing the birds.
Some children will compare how many birds they each have on
  their wires.
Some children will quantify how many birds they each have at the
  end of the game.

Modifications
Switch to larger birds and clothespins for younger children. They
  may find the larger size easier to manipulate.
For more advanced children, use one or two standard dice.

Questions to Extend Thinking
Do the wires have the same number of birds?
How many birds will you have if you get one more?
How many birds could sit on this wire?
If one bird flew away, how many would you have?

Integrated Curriculum Activities
Switch to a subtraction game ("Birds Fly Home," activity 5.11),
  after children have had many experiences adding birds.
Put bird nests in the science area (see *More Than Magnets*,
  activity 2.8).
Include feathers as a collage material in the art area.
Sing songs about birds (see *More Than Singing*, activity 2.2).
Read books about birds, such as *Good-Night Owl*, by Pat Hutchins
  (New York: Macmillan, 1972), *Owl Babies*, by Martin Waddell
  (Cambridge, MA: Candlewick, 1992), and *Flap Your Wings and
  Try*, by Charlotte Pomerantz (New York: Greenwillow, 1989).

Helpful Hints
Drill the holes in the
dowel to hold the wire
before gluing the dowels
to the base.

To further secure the
wire, wrap it around the
dowels and then secure
it in place with plastic
tape.

5.11 Birds Fly Home

Description

This follow-up game to "Birds on a Wire" focuses on subtraction. Children start by clipping 10 birds to the wire frames used in activity 5.10. They spin the bird spinner to determine how many birds fly home to their nest.

Math Concepts

▲ subtraction
▲ creation and comparison of sets
▲ quantification

Materials

▲ telephone pole frame, as described in activity 5.10
▲ small birds glued to tiny clothespins, as described in activity 5.10
▲ bird spinner, also described in activity 5.10
▲ 2 bird nests (approximately 3 inches in diameter) from a craft store, or 2 round baskets to use as nests

Child's Level
This activity is most appropriate for older preschool or kindergarten children.

What to Look For
Children will spin the spinner to determine how many birds to put in their nests.

Children will re-count the number of birds on the wire each time they have to subtract some birds.

Children will notice that as more birds are added to the nest, there are fewer on the wire.

Modification
For younger children, start with only five birds on the wire and a teacher-made die with only one or two dots per side.

Questions to Extend Thinking
How many birds will be left after these two fly away?

Do you have more birds in your nest or on your wire?

How many more birds are on this wire than on this wire?

If you get a two on the spinner, will you have any birds left on the wire?

Integrated Curriculum Activity
Change the words to the familiar "Ten in the Bed" song to correspond to this activity. This will encourage subtraction by one.

There were five on the wire, and the little bird said,
"I'm tired, I'm tired,"
So he flew back to the nest.

There were four on the wire...

Helpful Hints

Check craft stores or party supply stores for large bird nests. Round baskets are also suitable.

5.12 Shopping Cart Bonanza

Description

For this game, each player has a dollhouse-size shopping cart. Players take turns rolling a die and selecting tiny plastic foods to put in their carts.

Math Concepts

▲ creation and comparison of sets
▲ quantification
▲ addition

Materials

▲ 2 novelty shopping carts (approximately 3 inches long)
▲ tiny plastic foods
▲ a 1–3 or 1–6 die

Child's Level

This activity is appropriate for either preschool or kindergarten children.

What to Look For

Children will roll the die to determine how many items to place in their shopping carts.

Children will select a quantification strategy (global, one-to-one correspondence, or counting) commensurate with their level of thinking.

Some children will sort the food by categories and compare how many of each type they have.

Children will try to fill the shopping carts.

Modification

For kindergarten children, create a set of cards with a picture of a food and the name of the food written on each card. Children can draw a card to determine what type of food to take and then roll the die to find out how many they need to take. Some children may wish to graph the results.

Questions to Extend Thinking

How many pieces of food do you think will fit in your cart?
What kind of food do you have the most of?
Is there a way to find out which cart has the most food?

Integrated Curriculum Activities

Set up a grocery store in the dramatic play area.
Create a gross-motor version of the game with child-size shopping carts, plastic fruits and vegetables from dramatic play, and a large die to roll. Paint lines across the sidewalk to create a path (activity 1.16).

Helpful Hints

Look for tiny food items in novelty or party supply stores. The shopping carts may be found in the same type of store or with doll furniture in craft stores.

5.13 International Flags

Description

Children are intrigued with the color and design of flags. For this activity, children spin a spinner and add a corresponding number of international flags of their choice to a small pegboard. By the end of the game, each child has quite a collection.

Math Concepts

▲ quantification
▲ creation and comparison of sets
▲ addition

Materials

▲ 40 tiny novelty flags (approximately 3 inches tall)
▲ 2 wooden pegboards (approximately 6 inches square)
▲ flag spinner, made by drawing or stamping flag outlines onto a blank spinner in groups of 1 to 4

Child's Level

This activity is most appropriate for older preschool and kindergarten children.

What to Look For

Children will spin the spinner to determine how many flags to take.

Children will use a quantification strategy (global, one-to-one correspondence, or counting) commensurate with their level of thinking.

Some children will initially put flags onto their pegboards without regard to the number of flags on the spinner.

Some children will compare how many flags they each have.

Some children will sort the flags by color or design.

Modifications

Add a second attribute for children to consider besides quantity. Teachers can create a set of colored cards. For each turn, children can select a card to indicate a color that must be present in the flags they select and use the spinner to determine the number of flags to pick.

Include more flags in the game. Children can roll two dice and add the quantities together before selecting an equivalent number of flags.

Questions to Extend Thinking

How many flags do you have so far?

How many of your flags have stripes?

What color do you think appears on the most flags?

If you get two more flags, how many will you have?

Integrated Curriculum Activities

Read and sing the book *What Is Your Language?* by Debra Leventhal (New York: Dutton, 1994), which includes flags and children from around the world.

Make a flag memory game by copying flag designs onto index cards.

Encourage children to create their own flags by including index cards and colored pencils in the art area.

Helpful Hints

Flag specialty stores often have inexpensive sets of tiny flags. Check telephone directories or try browsing the Internet.

5.14 Upside-Down People Game

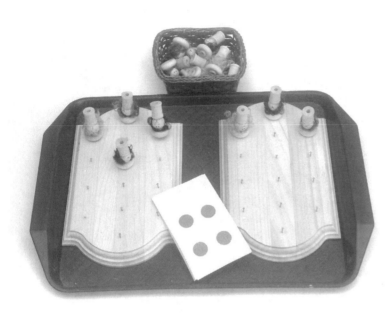

Description
Children are amused by the idea of topsy-turvy or upside-down people. This game includes spool people that fit upside down on a geoboard frame. Children draw cards to determine how many upside-down people to put on their board. This activity correlates well with the popular children's book *Silly Sally,* by Audrey Wood.

Math Concepts
▲ creation and comparison of sets
▲ quantification
▲ addition
▲ one-to-one correspondence

Materials
▲ 2 geoboards, made by hammering small nails into a wood base (approximately 9 by 5 inches)
▲ spool people, made by gluing macramé bead heads to spools and adding doll hair
▲ quantification cards, made from index cards with ½-inch stickers mounted in sets of 1 to 4

Child's Level
This activity is appropriate for both preschool and kindergarten children.

What to Look For

Some children will initially place one person on each peg of the geoboard without regard to the number of dots on the card. They are working on one-to-one correspondence relationships.

Children will draw cards to determine how many people to place on their geoboards.

Children will use a quantification strategy (global, one-to-one correspondence, or counting) commensurate with their level of thinking.

Some children may set the spool people directly on the circles on the cards to help them determine how many people to take.

Modification

For younger children, start with quantities of one to three on the cards.

Questions to Extend Thinking

How can you tell how many people to take?

How many more people do you need to finish this row?

How many people will you have if you get one more?

Integrated Curriculum Activities

Read the book *Silly Sally,* by Audrey Wood (New York: Harcourt, 1992).

Clap the beats of a "Silly Sally" chant for a rhythm activity (see *More Than Singing,* activity 3.9).

Create board games to correlate with *Silly Sally* (activities 6.1, 7.1a, and 7.1b).

Take photographs of the children doing upside-down tricks and make a class "Upside Down" book.

Some macramé beads already have faces, but they are more expensive. Faces can be drawn on plain macramé beads with permanent markers, or they can be painted on with acrylic paint.

Use a hot glue gun to glue the spools, beads, and hair together. A small piece of dowel inserted through the holes helps hold the pieces together securely.

5.15 Dinosaur War

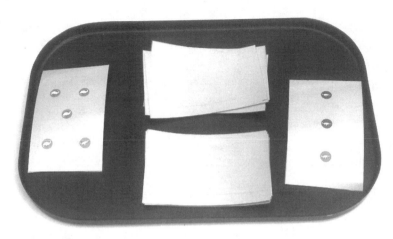

Description

Dinosaur War is a variation of the traditional card game War. The teacher-made playing cards consist of dinosaur stickers mounted on index cards. Each card has one to six dinosaurs on it. Children divide the cards among themselves before beginning the game. All of the players turn over a card simultaneously. The player with the largest number of dinosaurs on his or her card takes all of the cards from that round. Children can decide what to do if players turn over cards with an equivalent number of dinosaurs on them. When all of the cards have been used, children can determine how many cards each player has won. This game challenges children to constantly compare sets as they try to determine whose card has the most dinosaurs.

Math Concepts
▲ comparison of sets
▲ quantification
▲ division

Materials
▲ 40 to 50 dinosaur playing cards, made by adhering dinosaur stickers to green index cards with sets of 1 to 6 dinosaurs per card

Child's Level
This game is most appropriate for kindergarten children, since it is more difficult than most of the die and counter manipulative games.

What to Look For

Children will argue and discuss as they try to decide whose card has the most dinosaurs.

Children will quantify and compare how many cards they have at the end of the game.

Children will devise strategies for dividing the cards at the beginning of the game.

Modification

Once children have become adept at comparing sets of one to six dinosaurs, introduce additional cards with sets to ten.

Questions to Extend Thinking

Whose card has the most dinosaurs?

What should we do when we have a tie?

How can we tell which card has the most dinosaurs?

Integrated Curriculum Activities

Read books about dinosaurs, such as *Dinosaur, Dinosaur,* by Byron Barton (New York: Crowell, 1989) and *Digging Up Dinosaurs,* by Aliki (New York: Crowell, 1988).

Assemble a collection of small dinosaurs for sorting and classifying. (See *More Than Counting,* chapter 3, for information about collections.)

Clap dinosaur names for a rhythm activity (see *More Than Singing,* activity 3.2).

Add dinosaur word cards to the writing area.

Estimate how many children's feet will fit in a Tyrannosaurus rex footprint (activity 3.5).

Helpful Hints

Laminate the cards or cover them with clear contact paper to increase their durability.

More Grid Games

Claire and Maya burst into the classroom on a Monday morning. "Look, look! There's a new game!" Without even removing their coats, they sat down at the math game table and rolled the die, which was made with tiny apple stickers. Each girl had a basket of apple counters and a game board made with nine illustrations of apples. Claire rolled a three on the die and placed three flat wooden apples on each of three apple illustrations. Maya had already begun to place one wooden apple on each illustration of her board, without regard for the die.

Omeed and Sherein later came to the game table to find all eighteen wooden apples in one basket. The teacher asked if they could divide the apples so each child would have the same amount of apples. Omeed poured the apples onto the table and gave one to Sherein and one to himself until the apples had been evenly distributed.

▲ ▲ ▲

Children respond positively to math materials that do not have predetermined rules so that competition is not a major focus. When children have opportunities to think about mathematical problems in game situations, they often attempt to solve more difficult math problems than they would typically encounter. They may take more risks in thinking and learn to accept individual differences in approaching math problems. Teachers have numerous opportunities to stimulate thinking and assess mathematical understanding as children play grid games.

Teachers' Questions
What are grid games?

Grid games are unique, teacher-developed game boards used in combination with dice and counters. The game boards are configured to resemble a grid with varying quantities of spaces. The counters and dice coordinate with the topic of the game and contribute to the complexity of the game. Each child has a game board and counters, but typically children share the die or dice. Thus, while children are able to play the game in a noncompetitive manner, they are encouraged to communicate about mathematics as they encounter the viewpoint of another person playing the same game.

How do children play grid games?

Children play grid games in a variety of ways, depending on their age, experience, and understanding of quantification. Younger, less-experienced children may initially use the counters for pretend play, especially when the counters are small figures or objects, such as tiny squirrels or miniature foods. Children who are working on one-to-one correspondence relationships, but are not yet ready to quantify, may place one counter on each space of the grid, without using the die, to determine the quantity of counters needed. Eventually children begin to quantify and attempt to take the same number of counters as they roll on the die.

How do children quantify with grid games?

Children pass through Kamii's stages of quantification (see chapter 1): ***global, one-to-one correspondence,*** and ***counting.***[1] Children at the ***global*** stage may take a handful of counters or make a pile of counters that looks about the same as the quantity on the die. At the ***one-to-one correspondence*** stage, children may take a counter each time they point to a dot on the die in order to create an equivalent set. (Note that children who place one counter on each space of the grid, without regard for the quantity on the die, are exploring one-to-one correspondence, but not in relationship to quantification.) Children eventually employ ***counting*** as their method of quantification.

In order to count accurately, children must understand three of Gelman and Gallistel's counting principles: ***stable order counting*** (saying the number words in a consistent, accepted sequence), ***one-to-one correspondence*** (each object may be counted once and only once), and ***cardinality*** (the last number counted represents the total).[2] Children may choose counting as their method of quantification without fully understanding all of the counting principles. For example, a child may say she has twelve spaces on a ten-space grid because she double-counts some of the spaces. While she has constructed *cardinality,* she has not yet mastered the *one-to-one correspondence* concept, which eludes preschool children for an extended period of time.

Children will select the method of quantification that is best suited to their level of understanding in each specific situation.

They may revert to a less advanced stage when the quantities become larger. For example, a child who counts to determine the quantity of dots on a die may revert to the one-to-one correspondence stage when asked whether two children have the same amount of counters. Similarly, a child might divide a group of ten counters between two people by lining up the counters in two rows (one-to-one correspondence); however, when the quantities exceed ten, the same child may revert to the global stage and make two piles that appear to contain the same amount. Such shifts in quantification strategies may continue for a long time.

Why are grid games important to include in the curriculum?

Grid games provide opportunities for children to progress through the quantification stages and to develop the concepts necessary to play more complex games, such as short and long path games (discussed in chapter 7). Grid games are especially valuable tools for constructing the concepts of one-to-one correspondence and the comparison of sets. Young children are intrigued by the interesting design of grid game boards and the unique counters that coordinate with the games. They are eager to roll the die to create and compare sets. These experiences provide opportunities for children to construct mathematical concepts and higher-level thinking skills.

How are grid games different from path games?

Grid games encourage children to create one-to-one correspondence relationships with concrete objects. They are the easiest type of board game for young children to play. While path games encourage children to create and compare sets, they do not provide concrete objects for children to use when quantifying or creating one-to-one correspondence relationships. Each grid game contains two game boards, thus eliminating the need for children to share space. Grid games often have a teacher-made die, with fewer dots than a standard 1–6 die, to allow younger or less experienced children to be successful when quantifying. The games do not have a set of rules for play, so each child can play at an individual level. Children can play grid games in a parallel-play fashion or in cooperation with another child.

What are the easiest types of grid games?

The easiest grid games have relatively few spaces, the same number of counters as spaces on the grid boards, and a teacher-made 1–3 die. The game boards may be marked into eight or nine squares to clearly define the spaces and encourage children to create a one-to-one correspondence between the counters and the spaces on the grid. The die consists of a 1-inch cube with one, two, or three ¼-inch file folder dots on each side. The game boards and the counters should be exactly the same in design and color to eliminate any concerns children might have as they learn to cooperate when playing board games. Information about the level of difficulty for each grid game is included with the activities in this chapter.

What are the most difficult types of grid games?

Grid games that have many spaces, multiple counters, grid boards with unusual configurations, and dice with six or more dots are the most difficult for children to play. The level of difficulty of grid games increases as the quantity of spaces and counters rises. For example, a grid game with twelve spaces on each game board and twenty-four counters for each player is more difficult than a grid game with twelve spaces and twelve counters for each player. The use of a 1–6 die or a pair of regular dice also increases the difficulty of a grid game. Teachers should carefully design grid games based on observations of their class.

Why are grid games that correlate with other curriculum materials especially valuable?

Children are attracted to grid games that contain elements that are familiar to them, such as characters from a book, objects that correlate with the season, or materials related to the science or dramatic play areas. Repeated experience with the same or similar materials often leads to new and additional learning for children. Grid games that coordinate with other curriculum areas provide an immediate connection to previous knowledge. Thus, when children play a grid game based on the book *Owl Babies,* they may already be familiar with the story line and recognize the baby owls on the grid. After playing the grid game, children may wish to reread the book or use puppets to retell the story. This is an example of circular or integrated curriculum planning. The book stimulates interest in the grid game, which in turn encourages children to return to the book or puppets.

What is the teacher's role?

Teachers observe and document the interests and quantification levels of the children. They design and implement grid games based on these observations. Teachers may also serve as a play partner with children who wish to play math games. As the teacher plays or observes, she may ask questions to stimulate thinking or encourage children to reflect upon the strategies they use to quantify. Suggestions for questions to ask can be found with the activities in this chapter.

How can teachers create grid boards?

Teachers can design grid boards on a computer, draw the lines by hand, or photocopy a sample grid. Computer-generated grids give teachers the option of varying the size of the boxes as they experiment with the design of the game. The lines are always straight and perpendicular. Grids can be drawn using word processing software by constructing tables with borders. Teachers can also draw grids by hand. The trick is to make the lines straight and perpendicular without smearing the ink. A sample grid with fifteen spaces (three by five) is included in the appendix. Teachers can photocopy it to use it as a base for games. The size of the grids can be altered on a photocopy machine. The grid may be trimmed to produce grids of eight (two by four), nine (three by three), ten (two by five), or twelve (three by four) spaces.

Can children create their own grid games?

Yes! Children may spontaneously create grid games using other materials in the classroom. Teachers can provide specific materials, either as a special activity or as a component of the art area, to encourage children to design and make grid games. One-inch graph paper often sparks ideas for grid games. An 8- by 10-inch sheet of paper can be trimmed to the desired size for the game. The lines, which are already drawn on the paper, divide it into spaces similar to the teacher-made grid boards. A selection of beans, pasta wheels, or other small items may be used as the counters.

How do children benefit from designing their own grid games?

In addition to the exploration of creative ideas, children also benefit mathematically from designing their own grid games. As children use materials in unique ways, they further their creative development through flexible thinking, elaboration of ideas, and expression of thoughts. When children attempt to explain their grid games to others, they must think about the mathematics involved in the game. They already have some knowledge of grid games, based on their experiences with teacher-made games, which they attempt to apply to the games they design.

How can teachers assess mathematical knowledge as children play grid games?

Teachers observe children as they play the games, ask questions, and modify the games based on the information they collect. Many teachers keep a journal or log to document anecdotal information. Observations might include the child's level of quantification, understanding of one-to-one correspondence, and ability to create and compare sets of objects. Teachers may also wish to use the assessment form in the appendix.

Endnotes

1. Constance Kamii, *Number in Preschool and Kindergarten* (Washington, DC: NAEYC, 1982) 35.
2. Rochel Gelman and C. R. Gallistel, *The Child's Understanding of Number,* 2nd ed. (Cambridge, MA: Harvard UP, 1986) 79.

More Grid Game
Activities

6.1 Walking Upside Down

Thanks to Liz Van Fleet for this idea.

Description
Older preschool children often delight in silliness. This game coordinates with the book *Silly Sally*, by Audrey Wood, in which the characters walk backward and upside down. The spaces on the grid are made with upside-down rubber stamp impressions of a dog and a loon, two of the characters Silly Sally meets in the book. The spaces of the grid are also decorated with rubber stamp impressions of blades of grass and tiny flower stickers. The counters are large plastic shapes that look like flowers.

Math Concepts
▲ one-to-one correspondence
▲ creation and comparison of sets
▲ quantification

Materials
▲ 2 yellow grid boards (10 by 10 inches), each marked into 15 spaces
▲ rubber stamp impressions of a dog, a loon, and blades of grass
▲ tiny flower stickers
▲ 30 plastic or cloth flowers, large enough to cover the grid spaces
▲ a 1–4 die, made by adhering ¼-inch round file stickers to a 1-inch cube
▲ 2 small baskets for the counters

Child's Level
This game is most appropriate for older, more experienced preschool and kindergarten children. The extra decorations on the board may confuse younger children as they attempt to create a one-to-one correspondence relationship between the grid spaces and the counters.

What to Look For

Many children will roll the die, take an equivalent set of flower counters, and place one on each space of the grid.

Children will select a quantification strategy based on their level of development—global, one-to-one correspondence, or counting.

Some children may place one flower counter on each space of the grid without regard for the quantity on the die.

Some children may compare the quantities of flowers they each have.

Some children may choose to quantify the total amount of flowers on the two game boards.

Modifications

For older or more experienced children, use a pair of regular dice and sixty tiny flower erasers, enough for each child to place two on each space on the grid. This increases the difficulty of the game.

To simplify the game, eliminate the grass and the tiny flower stickers from the design of the game board. This reduces the amount of detail that might confuse younger children.

Questions to Extend Thinking

How many flowers will you need altogether to have one for each dog?

Do you each have the same number of flowers? How can you find out?

Do you have enough flowers to place two on each loon? (Ask this question if the game is modified to include thirty tiny flower erasers for each game board.)

Integrated Curriculum Activities

Include *Silly Sally,* by Audrey Wood (New York: Harcourt, 1992) in the reading area.

Graph the types of fasteners on the children's shoes (see *More Than Counting*, activity 6.3).

Plan a foot-printing activity on a long roll of shelf paper.

Design manipulative, short, and long path games on the same topic (activities 5.14, 7.1a, and 7.1b).

6.2 Baby Owls

Description
Many teachers like to explore birds with their classes. This game coordinates with the book *Owl Babies,* by Martin Waddell. The game boards consist of rubber stamp impressions of an owl on computer-generated grids. The grids are duplicated on buff-colored paper to simulate the coloring of the owls, mounted on black poster board, and laminated. The counters are flat, white marble chips.

Math Concepts
▲ one-to-one correspondence
▲ creation and comparison of sets
▲ quantification

Materials
▲ 2 computer-generated or hand-drawn grids, each with 12 spaces, duplicated on buff-colored paper and mounted on black poster board (8 by 7 inches)
▲ rubber stamp of an owl, to create an owl impression on each space of the grid
▲ 24 flat, white marble chips
▲ 2 small baskets for the counters
▲ a 1–3 die

Child's Level

This game is most appropriate for children who are working on quantification from one to three and are beginning to understand one-to-one correspondence.

What to Look For

Many children will roll the die, take an equivalent number of counters, and place one on each space of the grid.

Children will select a quantification strategy based on their level of development—global, one-to-one correspondence, or counting.

Some children may place one counter on each grid space without regard for the quantity on the die.

Some children may place more than one counter on each space of the grid.

Modifications

Use small owls as counters to represent the mother owl, so that each baby owl has a mother owl.

To increase the difficulty of the game, use one or two regular dice and twenty-four counters for each player. They can place two counters on each space of the grid.

Questions to Extend Thinking

Do you each have the same number of owls on your grid?

What do you have to roll on the die to fill the last spaces of the grid?

If you roll a two, will your board be full?

Integrated Curriculum Activities

Include books about owls, such as *Owl Babies,* by Martin Waddell (Cambridge, MA: Candlewick, 1992) and *Good-Night Owl,* by Pat Hutchins (New York: Macmillan, 1972), in the reading area.

Design short and long path owl games for the math area (activities 7.2a and 7.2b).

Use owl-shaped cookie cutters as printing tools for an art activity.

Sing songs about birds (see *More Than Singing,* activity 2.2).

Put bird nests in the science area for children to examine (see *More Than Magnets,* activity 2.8).

Helpful Hints

Use yellow paper for duplication of the grid if buff paper is not available.

6.3 Pirate Treasure

Description

This game coordinates with the book *Tough Boris*, by Mem Fox. Many children are drawn to the story of the fearless pirate, who also cries when he is sad. The colorful jewels and shiny pirate stickers attract children to the game.

Math Concepts

▲ one-to-one correspondence
▲ creation and comparison of sets
▲ quantification

Materials

▲ 2 black grid boards (10 by 4 inches), each marked into 14 spaces with a silver metallic paint marker
▲ 28 pirate stickers, to place in the grid boxes
▲ 28 novelty jewels
▲ a 1–4 die, made with silver dots on a black, 1-inch cube
▲ 2 small treasure boxes for the jewels

Child's Level

This game is most appropriate for children who have had some experience playing grid games with fewer spaces and who can quantify using a 1–3 die.

What to Look For

Many children will roll the die, take an equivalent set of jewels, and place one on each space of the grid.

Children will select a quantification strategy based on their level of development—global, one-to-one correspondence, or counting.

Some children may play with the treasure without regard for the grid game. They may compare quantities of jewels they each have.

Some children may ask for more jewels for the pirate.

Modifications

For older or more experienced children, use a pair of regular dice and fifty-six jewels. Each player can place two jewels on each space of the grid.

Place all of the jewels in one treasure box to encourage children to divide them equally before the game begins.

Substitute very large plastic jewels for children who have physical or cognitive delays (activity 8.5).

Comments and Questions to Extend Thinking

How many fewer jewels do I have than you?

How many more jewels do I need to cover all my spaces?

I have two spaces left. Do I have to roll two on the die?

How many jewels do we need for each pirate to have one?

Integrated Curriculum Activities

Include *Tough Boris,* by Mem Fox (New York: Harcourt, 1994) in the reading area.

Assemble a collection of jewels for sorting and classifying (see *More Than Counting,* activity 3.11).

Encourage children to estimate how many rings will fit on each finger of a small glove (activity 3.8).

Design pirate path games for the math area (activities 7.3a and 7.3b).

Put small boats in the water table. Children can experiment with how many jewels it takes to sink them (see *More Than Magnets,* activity 4.14).

Craft or fabric stores sell small jewels for decorating clothing.

For variety, use parrot erasers instead of jewels for the counters.

6.4 The Spider and the Fly

Description
Young children respond readily to stories with a repeating text. This game coordinates with the predictable book *The Very Busy Spider,* by Eric Carle. In the story, a spider continues to spin her web as different farm animals invite her to join them. After all the animals pass by and the web is finished, the spider catches the "pesky fly." The spaces on the grid are made with a rubber stamp impression of a spider. The counters are plastic flies.

Math Concepts
▲ one-to-one correspondence
▲ creation and comparison of sets
▲ quantification

Materials
▲ 2 computer-generated or hand-drawn grids, each with 15 spaces, duplicated on white paper and mounted on green poster board (5½ by 8 inches)
▲ rubber stamp of a spider
▲ 30 plastic flies
▲ a 1–3 die
▲ 2 small baskets for the counters

Child's Level
This game is most appropriate for preschool or kindergarten children who are working on quantification to three.

What to Look For

Many children will roll the die, take an equivalent set of plastic flies, and place one on each space of the grid.

Children will select a quantification strategy based on their level of development—global, one-to-one correspondence, or counting.

Some children may roll the die and randomly place the flies onto the grid spaces.

Some children may place more than one plastic fly onto each space of the grid.

Some children may play with the plastic flies without regard for the mathematical aspects of the game until they have had more opportunities to play math games with partners.

Modifications

To increase the difficulty of the game, use one or two regular dice and more fly counters. Children can place multiple flies on each spider.

For variety, substitute small rubber farm animals for the counters.

Questions to Extend Thinking

How many flies do you have altogether?

How do you know how many flies to take?

How many flies have the spiders caught so far?

How many more flies do you need for every spider to have one?

Integrated Curriculum Activities

Include *The Very Busy Spider,* by Eric Carle (New York: Philomel, 1984) in the reading area.

Design spider path and collection games for the math area (activities 7.4a and 7.4b).

Introduce spider manipulative games (activities 5.3 and 5.4).

Take a walk with the children to look for spider webs. Mist the webs with a spray bottle of water so children can see the webs better.

Small plastic flies can be found in many party supply and cake decorating stores.

6.5 Colorful Mice

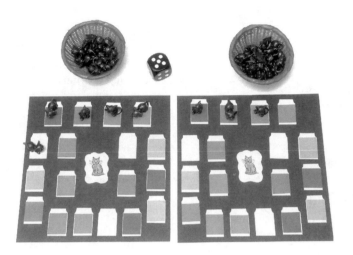

Description

Children are excited to discover that they can mix primary colors to create new colors. This game coordinates with the book *Mouse Paint,* by Ellen Stohl Walsh. In the story, small mice investigate pots of colorful paint. They eventually mix the primary colors to make new colors. The mice are always aware of the gray cat that may be close by, ready to pounce on them. To help children associate the math game with the book, a cat illustration is included in the middle of paint pots on the grid boards. Tiny mice are used for the counters. The cat adds a possible problem to solve since a counter for the cat is *not* included in the game pieces. The children may discuss whether they have enough counters for all the illustrations on the game board.

Math Concepts

▲ one-to-one correspondence
▲ creation and comparison of sets
▲ quantification
▲ division of materials

Materials

▲ 2 black grids (8 by 8½ inches), each with 18 small paint-pot illustrations (3 each of red, yellow, blue, green, orange, and purple) and 1 cat illustration, as pictured above
▲ 36 small plastic mice
▲ a 1–6 die
▲ basket for the mice counters

Child's Level

This game is most appropriate for older preschool and kindergarten children who have had many experiences playing grid games with a less complex design and fewer spaces.

What to Look For

Many children will roll the die, take an equivalent set of mice, and place one on each paint-pot illustration.

Children will select a quantification strategy based on their level of development—global, one-to-one correspondence, or counting.

Some children may include the cat as one of the grid spaces and discuss whether they have enough counters for all the illustrations.

Some children may ignore the cat illustration.

Modifications

Eliminate the cat illustration for a less complex grid.

For a simpler version of the grid, reduce the grid spaces to six, include only six mice, and use a 1–3 teacher-made die.

Questions to Extend Thinking

How can you divide the mice so that we each have the same amount?

Do you have the same number of each color of paint pot?

How many paint pots still need mice?

If the cat caught a mouse, how many would be left?

Integrated Curriculum Activities

Include *Mouse Paint,* by Ellen Stohl Walsh (New York: Harcourt, 1989) in the reading area.

Design color-related path games for the math area (activities 7.5a and 7.5b).

Plan color-mixing activities in the art area.

Sing songs about mice (see *More Than Singing,* activity 6.10).

Read other books about mixing colors, such as *Color Dance,* by Ann Jonas (New York: Greenwillow, 1989) and *Little Blue and Little Yellow,* by Leo Lionni (New York: Astor-Honor, 1993).

Helpful Hints

Use ¾-inch press-on dots for the grid boards if the paint pots are difficult to draw.

6.6 Tumbling Alphabet

Description

Generations of children have chanted traditional rhymes. This game coordinates with a book based on such a rhyme— *Chicka Chicka Boom Boom,* by Bill Martin, Jr., and John Archambault. In this pre-dictable book, the letters of the alphabet climb up a coconut tree. The palm tree stickers and alphabet counters help children associate the grid game with the book.

Math Concepts

▲ one-to-one correspondence
▲ creation and comparison of sets
▲ quantification

Materials

▲ 2 white grid boards (10½ by 10½ inches), with a border made of 1-inch strips of fluorescent pink paper decorated with orange dots
▲ 18 palm tree illustrations, to put in the grid spaces
▲ 18 or more alphabet letters (plastic, wood, or rubber)
▲ a 1–6 die

Child's Level

This game is most appropriate for older preschool children. Younger children may focus on the letters in their name and disregard the math component of the game.

What to Look For

Some children may initially talk about the letters and discuss whose name begins with each letter.

Many children will roll the die, take an equivalent set of alphabet letters, and place one on each coconut tree.

Children will select a quantification strategy based on their level of development—global, one-to-one correspondence, or counting.

Some children may place one letter on each coconut tree without regard for the die. They are focusing on one-to-one correspondence.

Modifications

Use buckeye nuts or filbert nuts as the counters, especially if children focus only on the letters of the alphabet. The nuts resemble coconuts.

For older children, use two dice and enough letters for each child to place two on each space of the grid.

Comments and Questions to Extend Thinking

Do you have enough letters to place one on each coconut tree?

How many letters do you need if you want two letters for each coconut tree?

If you roll a two, will each tree have a letter?

I see one letter on each tree on your board. I still have three empty trees.

Integrated Curriculum Activities

Include *Chicka Chicka Boom Boom,* by Bill Martin, Jr., and John Archambault (New York: Simon, 1989) in the reading area.

Display coconuts in the science area. Children can guess what's inside before opening the coconuts (see *More Than Magnets,* activity 2.10).

Sing songs that focus on letters, such as a version of "Bingo" that incorporates the children's names (see *More Than Singing,* activity 2.11).

Read other alphabet books, such as *Navajo ABC,* by Luci Tapahonso (New York: Simon, 1995), *A Is for Aloha,* by Stephanie Feeney (Honolulu: UP of Hawaii, 1980), and *K Is for Kiss Goodnight,* by Jill Sardegna (New York: Bantam, 1994).

Use hollow coconut shells as rhythm instruments (see *More Than Singing,* activity 4.8).

Office supply stores often stock plastic alphabet letters for display cases. Party supply stores often carry rubber erasers.

Use a hole punch to create orange circles for the border of the game boards.

6.7 Grandma's Cookies

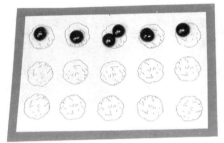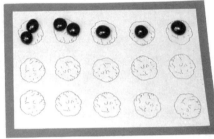

Description

Virtually all children are interested in cookies. This game coordinates with the book *The Doorbell Rang,* by Pat Hutchins. Two children have twelve cookies to divide until the doorbell rings and more children arrive. This continues until Grandma brings a tray full of cookies. In this cookie game, children use black marble chips to represent chocolate chips in the cookies on their game boards. They can add two dice together to determine how many chips to take.

Math Concepts

▲ one-to-one correspondence
▲ creation and comparison of sets
▲ quantification
▲ addition
▲ repeated addition, or multiplication

Materials

▲ 2 computer-generated or hand-drawn grids on light brown paper, each with 15 spaces, mounted on brown poster board (7 by 10½ inches); cookie illustrations are drawn in each space
▲ 60 to 90 black marble chips to use as chocolate chips
▲ two 1–6 dice

Child's Level

This game is most appropriate for kindergarten children who can quantify using a pair of regular dice and have had many experiences playing grid games. The inclusion of more than one counter for each grid space and the use of a pair of dice make this a more complex game.

What to Look For

Many children will roll the dice, take an equivalent amount of marble chips, and place one on each cookie on the grid.

Children will select a quantification strategy based on their level of development—global, one-to-one correspondence, or counting.

Some children will roll the dice, take an equivalent amount of marble chips, and place more than one chip on each cookie on the grid.

Some children may quantify the dots on each die and place an equivalent number of chips on an individual cookie.

Some children may use repeated addition to determine whether they have enough counters to place two on each space of the grid.

Modifications

For less experienced children, reduce the number of marble chips to sixteen, exactly enough to place one on each space of the grid.

Substitute Duplo people for the marble chips. Encourage children to find out if there are enough cookies for each person to have one.

Questions to Extend Thinking

Do you have enough chips to put two on each cookie? How many more would you need to put three on each cookie?

How can you divide the chips so that each person has the same amount?

Do all of the cookies have the same number of chips?

Which cookie has the fewest chips?

Integrated Curriculum Activities

Include *The Doorbell Rang,* by Pat Hutchins (New York: Greenwillow, 1986) in the reading area.

Assemble twelve toy people and twelve marble chips so that children can reenact the story of *The Doorbell Rang* (see *More Than Counting,* activity 2.26).

Design cookie path games (activities 7.7a and 7.7b).

Bake chocolate chip cookies with the children.

Let children vote on their favorite type of cookie and graph the results.

Set up a bakery in the dramatic play area (activity 1.1).

Sing a counting song about cookies (activity 5.6).

Helpful Hints

Trace a cookie from a package if a rubber stamp is not available.

6.8 Construction Zone

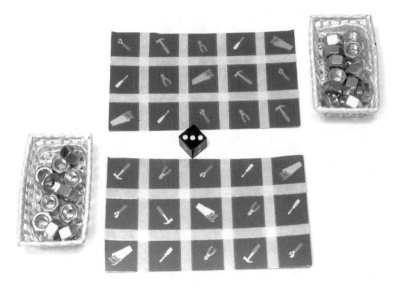

Thanks to René Freppon.

Description

This game coordinates well with a construction unit. The dramatic play area can be set up as a work site, with hard hats, pretend tools, and golf tees to hammer into Styrofoam. The grid boards for this game consist of tool stickers with hardware nuts for counters.

Math Concepts

▲ one-to-one correspondence
▲ creation and comparison of sets
▲ quantification

Materials

▲ 2 dark blue grid boards (10 by 5½ inches), each with 15 tool stickers
▲ ½-inch diameter yellow tape to make the grid lines on the board
▲ thirty 1-inch diameter hardware nuts to use as counters
▲ small wooden box or basket to store the counters
▲ a 1–3 die

Child's Level

This game is most appropriate for preschool or kindergarten children who can quantify using a 1–3 die and have had some previous experience using grid games.

What to Look For

Many children will roll the die, take an equivalent number of nuts, and place one on each tool on the grid board.

Children will select a quantification strategy based on their level of development—global, one-to-one correspondence, or counting.

Some children may roll the die, take an equivalent set of counters, and place all of them on one space of the grid.

Children may compare the amount of counters they each have.

Some children may place one nut on each space of the grid without regard for the quantity on the die. They are working on one-to-one correspondence.

Modifications

For more experienced children, use a pair of regular dice and sixty washers for counters. Children can stack two washers on each space of the grid board.

For variety, use two types of counters, such as wing nuts and washers, so that each player has fifteen wing nuts and fifteen washers.

Questions to Extend Thinking

How do you know how many nuts to take when you roll the die?

If you roll a three on the die, will all your grid spaces be filled?

Do you have just as many washers as wing nuts? How can you find out?

Integrated Curriculum Activities

Design construction path games for the math area (activities 7.8a and 7.8b).

Plan woodworking activities for your class.

Take a field trip to a construction site. Be sure to watch from a safe area.

Put word cards with the names of tools or types of trucks in the writing area.

Add trucks to the block area.

Read construction books, such as *Bam Bam Bam,* by Eve Merriam (New York: Scholastic, 1994), *Machines At Work,* by Byron Barton (New York: Harper, 1987), and *Skyscraper Going Up,* by Vicki Cobb (New York: Crowell, 1987).

Helpful Hints

If necessary, cut the handle of the hammer sticker shorter to make it fit into the same size grid space as the other tools.

6.9 Taking Care of Baby

Description

This game coordinates with a baby unit, which many teachers plan when children in the group experience the birth of a sibling. Other children in the class often have younger siblings and may remember the birth of a new baby. The teacher may set up the dramatic play area as a baby nursery with extra dolls, a changing table, bottles, blankets, and rattles. In this math game, children can collect bottles and pacifiers to distribute to the babies on their grid boards.

Math Concepts

▲ one-to-one correspondence
▲ creation and comparison of sets
▲ quantification
▲ division of a set
▲ repeated addition, or multiplication

Materials

▲ 2 light blue grids (8½ by 8½ inches), each with 15 baby stickers
▲ 30 small plastic baby bottles
▲ 30 small pacifiers
▲ 2 small baskets, to hold the counters
▲ a 1–6 die

Child's Level

This game is most appropriate for older preschool or kindergarten children who are able to quantify to six and have had numerous experiences playing grid games with only one counter for each grid space.

What to Look For

Many children will roll the die to determine how many bottles or
bears to take. They may attempt to collect one bottle and one
teddy bear for each baby.

Children will select a quantification strategy based on their level of
development—global, one-to-one correspondence, or counting.

Some children may roll the die, take an equivalent set of counters,
and place them all on one space of the grid.

Some children may roll the die, take an equivalent set of bottles,
and place one counter on each space of the grid.

Some children may use repeated addition to determine whether
they have enough counters to place two on each space of
the grid.

Modifications

For less experienced children, use one type of counter.

For kindergarten children, place all the counters in one basket. Ask
them to graph the results of the baby items they collect.

Questions to Extend Thinking

Do you have enough bottles and teddy bears to give each baby a
bottle and a bear?

How many more bears do you need to give each baby a bear?

Do we each have the same number of bottles? How do you know?

How many bottles do you need to give each baby two bottles?

Integrated Curriculum Activities

Design baby path games (activities 7.9a and 7.9b).

Sing baby songs (see *More Than Singing*, activities 2.1, 2.9, 2.12,
and 2.13).

Listen to a recording of lullabies from around the world, such as
"The World Sings Goodnight" (Silver Wave Records, SC 803).

Have children taste baby foods and vote on their favorites. Graph
the results at group time.

Wash baby clothes in the water table. Children can hang them up
to dry on a clothesline stretched between two pulleys (see *More
Than Magnets*, activity 4.16).

Read books about babies, such as *Hush!* by Minfong Ho (New
York: Orchard, 1996) and *Sleep, Sleep, Sleep,* by Nancy Van Laan
(Boston: Little, Brown, 1995).

Helpful Hints

Small baby items can be
found in cake decorat-
ing, party supply, or
craft stores.

6.10 Let's Go Shopping

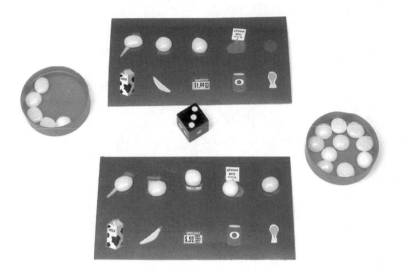

Description

This game coordinates with a grocery store unit, common in preschool and kindergarten curriculums. Most children are familiar with shopping in a grocery store or market. Many children have helped parents select the food to purchase. They quickly recognize the grocery store foods on the grid boards of this game.

Math Concepts

▲ one-to-one correspondence
▲ creation and comparison of sets
▲ quantification

Materials

▲ 2 dark blue grid boards (8 by 4½ inches), each with 10 stickers of different kinds of food found in a grocery store
▲ 20 white marble chips
▲ a 1–3 die
▲ 2 small baskets, for the counters

Child's Level

This game is most appropriate for children who are beginning to understand one-to-one correspondence and are working on quantification to three. The grid boards have a small number of items and exactly one counter for each item on the board.

What to Look For

Many children will roll the die, take an equivalent set of counters, and put one on each space of the grid.

Children will select a quantification strategy based on their level of development—global, one-to-one correspondence, or counting.

Some children may talk about the food items on the grid board without thinking about the mathematical aspects of the game until they have had more opportunities to play math games with partners.

Some children may place one marble chip on each sticker, without regard for the die. They are focusing on one-to-one correspondence.

Modifications

If children have difficulty creating a one-to-one correspondence relationship between the stickers and the counters, use a paint marker to draw clearly defined boxes around the stickers.

For more advanced children, switch to two regular dice and use pennies for the counters. The children can decide how many pennies each food item should cost.

Comments and Questions to Extend Thinking

How many counters can you take when you roll the die? (Use this question to focus the child's attention on the use of the die.)

I rolled a two. I can cover two things. (Use this comment to model rolling the die to quantify when it is your turn to play.)

Do we each have the same number of counters?

Integrated Curriculum Activities

Include books, such as *The Supermarket,* by Anne and Harlow Rockwell (New York: Macmillan, 1979) and *Feast for Ten,* by Cathryn Falwell (New York: Clarion, 1993), in the reading area.

Design other grocery store games for the math area (activities 5.12, 7.10a, and 7.10b).

Set up a grocery store in the dramatic play area.

Take a field trip to a grocery store. Children can dictate stories based on the experience.

Helpful Hints

Substitute pictures cut from coupons if stickers are not available.

6.11 Quilt Squares

Description

Many young children are fond of a favorite blanket or quilt. This game coordinates with a unit based on quilt books, such as *The Quilt,* by Ann Jonas, *Luka's Quilt,* by Georgia Guback, and *The Quilt Story,* by Tony Johnston. The game boards contain stickers of quilts and the counters are spools of thread.

Math Concepts

▲ one-to-one correspondence
▲ creation and comparison of sets
▲ quantification

Materials

▲ 2 black grids (8 by 8 inches), each with 16 quilt stickers
▲ 32 tiny wooden spools, wrapped with embroidery thread
▲ 2 small baskets for the counters
▲ a 1–3 die

Child's Level

This game is most appropriate for preschool or kindergarten children who are working on one-to-one correspondence and quantification to three.

What to Look For

Some children may roll the die, take an equivalent set of spools, and place one on each space of the grid.

Children will select a quantification strategy based on their level of development—global, one-to-one correspondence, or counting.

Some children may place one spool on each space of the grid, without regard for the die. They are focusing on one-to-one correspondence.

Some children may compare the quantities of spools they each have.

Some children may stack the spools of thread.

Modifications

If children have difficulty creating a one-to-one correspondence because more than one tiny spool will fit into each grid space, use larger spools of thread.

To increase the difficulty of the game, use a 1–6 die and more spools.

To add the possibility of patterning, use four different colors of thread with four spools of each color.

Questions to Extend Thinking

Do you have a spool of thread for each quilt?

How many more spools of thread do you need to cover the rest of your quilts?

Do you have just as many yellow spools of thread as you have red spools?

Integrated Curriculum Activities

Include *The Quilt,* by Ann Jonas (New York: Greenwillow, 1984), *Luka's Quilt,* by Georgia Guback (New York: Greenwillow, 1994), and *The Quilt Story,* by Tony Johnston (New York: Scholastic, 1985) in the reading area.

Design quilt path games for the math area (activities 7.11a and 7.11b).

Let children create class quilts (see *More Than Painting,* activities 7.5, 7.6, 7.7, and 7.16).

Encourage children to bring their own blankets and quilts to share with the class.

Helpful Hints

Fabric stores may sell tiny spools of thread in a variety of colors.

CHAPTER 7

More Path Games

Wesley and Isaac used a ten-sided die with a farm long path game. Wesley selected the pig as his mover, while Isaac chose the horse. This was the first time the boys, both five, used a die with more than six dots, although both of them could already combine the quantities on a pair of regular dice. Wesley looked ahead on the game and noticed that the path crossed a pond, a bridge, and a hay wagon. He suggested that if either of them landed on the pond, bridge, or wagon, he would lose a turn. They agreed. Wesley quickly counted the spaces to the first trap, the pond, and said, "I don't want to get a ten this time or I'll be stuck in the pond."

▲ ▲ ▲

Bianca and Ciara chose an owl long path game when they arrived at school. Brianna, Bianca's younger sister, watched them play. The older girls suggested that she roll the dice for them. Although she was not yet three years old, Brianna recognized the quantities one and two on the die. When the older girls finished the game, Brianna asked her mother to play with her. She imitated the way the girls rolled the dice and acted excited each time. Brianna jumped her mover from start to finish. The teacher asked her if she wanted to play another game and showed her the shorter version of the owl game. Brianna again recognized the quantities one and two on the die. She moved one space on the first roll, one space on the second roll, and then jumped to the end!

▲ ▲ ▲

Path games typically attract children at many different levels of development. Younger siblings want to join in the play with big brothers and sisters; older children often model higher-level thinking strategies for younger or less experienced children. When peers play together, they may have to explain the reasoning behind the choices they make. Teachers and parents have numerous opportunities to observe progressions in thinking, note the mistakes that naturally occur, and ask children questions to stimulate further thinking. Teacher-developed path games are designed to meet the needs of individuals as well as specific groups. Since children play them in a variety of ways, they are self-leveling games.

Teachers' Questions
What are path games?

Path games are similar to commercial board games, such as Candyland *and* Chutes and Ladders. *They have a path made of dots or squares, movers for each player, and dice to determine how many spaces the players may advance.* Teacher-developed path games, however, are carefully designed to

▲ incorporate current research on how children construct mathematical knowledge;

▲ build on the knowledge previously constructed by children;

▲ meet the developmental needs of the group;

▲ provide self-leveling math activities;

▲ make connections to other high-interest curriculum materials; and

▲ provide opportunities for teacher assessment of mathematical thinking.

Why are path games important to include in the curriculum?

Path games encourage children to use thinking strategies already developed through interactions with math manipulatives and grid games, but at a more advanced level. While children continue to apply concepts that involve one-to-one correspondence and the comparison of sets, there is less emphasis on using concrete objects to quantify. Path games use the familiar dice of other math activities, but they require children to think more abstractly when they move along a path according to the quantity on the dice. For example, when a child plays a math manipulative game such as the "Elephant Stacking Game" (activity 5.1) and rolls *six* on a die, she takes six square tiles to place on top of the elephant. Similarly, when a child plays a grid game and rolls a *six*, she places six concrete objects on the grid board. However, when a child plays a path game and rolls *six* on a die, she does not have six concrete objects to quantify. More abstract thinking is needed to conceptualize *six* among all the spaces of the path.

Path games that incorporate the use of a pair of dice encourage children to think about addition. Before they fully understand the concept of addition, children often count one die and move accordingly before counting the second die and moving again. They do not yet view the separate amounts as two parts of a whole quantity. When children begin to understand that the two quantities can be combined to make the total, they count all the dots. Eventually children begin to "add on." For example, if a child rolls *five* and *seven,* he mentally quantifies seven on one die and continues on from seven as he counts the dots on the other die, saying, "7—8, 9, 10, 11, 12." Some children may also think about subtraction, multiplication, and division as they explore path games. The activities in this chapter contain information about the types of math concepts children may construct when playing the games.

What levels of quantification emerge as children play path games?

Teachers may observe children at the global, one-to-one correspondence, and counting levels of quantification when they play path games. This is especially true when children are in multiage groupings. Children generally choose activities and math games at a level close to their developmental stage. Although children may express initial interest in a path game, they often select a more developmentally appropriate activity if the path game is too difficult.

Global—Younger or less experienced children, who may not be developmentally ready to play path games, often approach them in a pretend play fashion. They may play with the movers or talk about the illustrations on the board and completely disregard the die. While some children may be able to determine the quantity on the die, they may hop randomly along the path. This is similar to children who roll the die and take a handful of counters when playing grid games. They are using a less logical approach to quantification than in subsequent stages.

One-to-one correspondence—Many children advance to the second stage of quantification and apply this knowledge to path games. For example, a child who rolls *three* on a die may advance one space each time she points to a dot on the die until she has moved three spaces.

Counting—Path games are usually intended for children who are already at the third level of quantification. Children at this level decide how many spaces to advance by first counting the dots on the die and then moving an equivalent number of spaces along the path. While these children may continue to make errors in counting, such as double-counting or skipping spaces on the path, they are becoming more accurate in quantifying and have a more logical approach to quantification than children at the earlier stages. Some children no longer re-count the space they already occupy when they take a subsequent turn. Children at the counting stage eventually develop accuracy in counting and may begin to understand addition, including remembering the combinations on a pair of regular dice.

Why is there a need for teacher-developed path games?

Many commercial board games do not provide enough opportunities for children at a variety of developmental levels to play the games. The games may be either too easy or too confusing, and they come with rules that preclude self-leveling play. These obstacles may inhibit the construction of higher-level thinking and may prevent some children from playing the games. Teachers can design a variety of path games to encourage all children to play in ways best suited to their level of thinking. Teacher-made games may also encourage children to use higher-level thinking strategies.

What are the easiest path games?

*The easiest path games are **short path** games, which children typically can play after considerable experience playing grid games.* They are intended as a bridge between grid games and the more difficult long path games. The path, which contains ten to twelve spaces, is straight to help eliminate confusion and encourage children to move one space for each dot on the die. Since each child has his own path, problems associated with sharing space and remembering which mover to use are avoided. This allows children to focus on the mathematical aspects of the game. A single 1–3 die is used to encourage turn taking and the exchange of ideas, which becomes even more important at a later time when children play long path games. Some short path games have objects for children to collect each time they reach the end of the path. However, the easiest short path games do not include collection pieces because inexperienced children are likely to perceive the path as a grid and place one object on each space of the path.

What are the most difficult path games?

*The most complex path games are **long path** games, which usually contain twenty-five or more spaces.* The players share a common path that often curves into an S-formation on the game board. The most difficult long path games contain at least thirty-five spaces, have a more complex path configuration, and include trap or bonus spaces. They incorporate a pair of regular dice. More complex long path games are introduced after children have had numerous opportunities to play less-difficult path games that have fewer spaces, a very clear path, a single 1–6 die, and no elaborate trap or bonus spaces.

What should teachers consider when creating path games?

Teachers should consider the age and experience of the children in the group to eliminate problems that might result from errors in design. When making path games, teachers might ask themselves the following questions:

Is the mover smaller than the spaces on the path? (This helps children visualize the space their mover is occupying.)
Are the spaces far enough apart so that children can clearly perceive the individual spaces on the path?
For long path games, are the movers different from each other so that children can distinguish which mover is theirs? (Movers for short path games can be identical since the players have separate paths.)
Is the game board attractive? (Children are more motivated to play games that are aesthetically pleasing.)
Is the game durable? (Math games usually get a lot of use.)
Is the number of dots on the dice commensurate with the difficulty level of the game? (Short path games typically incorporate a 1–3 die, while one or more 1–6 dice are used with long path games.)
Do the movers coordinate with the subject of the game?

Why are path games that coordinate with other curriculum materials especially valuable?

Children are intrigued by path games that coordinate with other curriculum materials, such as high-interest books, dramatic play themes, and seasonal changes. Children are likely to be drawn to a path game with a popular theme. For example, they may associate illustrations on a game board with a familiar book, such as an upside-down silhouette used to represent the main character in *Silly Sally* (activity 7.1a). A collection of grocery items used in conjunction with a path game (activity 7.10b) may remind children of a grocery store in the dramatic play area. Games associated with familiar or popular topics may encourage children who might otherwise avoid math materials to repeatedly return to the games. Conversely, children who enjoy the math games may be motivated to explore other curricular materials related to the games, such as dramatic play props or specific books.

What is the teacher's role?

In addition to designing appropriate games based on the interests and developmental levels of the children, teachers can stimulate higher-level thinking through appropriate modeling and specific questioning techniques. When playing math games with children, teachers can encourage the development of mathematical thinking by modeling mathematical strategies at or slightly above the child's level of thinking. For example, if the child hops the mover randomly from start to finish, the teacher, while taking his turn, may verbally describe rolling the dice and moving an equivalent number of spaces. If the child does not yet *add on* when counting, the teacher might model that strategy when it is his turn. Suggested questions and comments to extend thinking can be found in the activities in this chapter.

Why should teachers avoid correcting thinking errors made by children?

Thinking errors are a natural part of the process of the construction of mathematical knowledge. They provide the teacher with valuable information for determining questions to ask or future games to design. Telling children how to solve a problem does not result in a change in their thinking. While they may follow the teacher's suggestions, they have not yet constructed the underlying concepts. Also, if children are told how to quantify, they may be less willing to take risks in mathematical problem solving and may decide that only the teacher knows how to quantify accurately. Although teachers should not correct the errors children make, other children may be anxious to describe where mistakes have been made. This often causes less experienced children to rethink their method of play. After many opportunities to play math games, listen to other children's thinking strategies, or observe the teacher modeling a higher level of mathematical understanding, children construct the necessary knowledge to move forward in thinking.

How can teachers encourage children to design their own path games?

Teachers can plan a special activity for children to design math games. Many early childhood programs have a group or circle time as a planned part of each day. This is a perfect opportunity to suggest the possibility that children can make math games for the classroom. The materials needed for the games can be displayed in a special place with a teacher available to assist children with problems they may encounter.

What materials are needed in order for children to design path games?

Children need materials to create a game board, movers, and dice. Stiff paper or poster board and press-on dots allow children to create a path for the game. They may also need colored pencils or markers to decorate the board or write instructions. Wooden spools or other materials can be used to make movers; 1-inch cubes and file folder stickers can be used to make dice. Children familiar with teacher-made path games will recognize these materials and be able to design games. They often ask for additional materials as they plan the design. Teachers can supply construction paper, glue, toothpicks, fancy stickers, tape, and other materials as needed. This project may require more than one day!

How do children benefit as they design path games?

The process of designing games and communicating to others how to play them forces children to think about quantification and consider the viewpoint of others. Children who are experienced game players understand the basic design of path games. They must consider how many dots they need to make the path, the configuration of the path, the trap or bonus spaces, and what kind of dice to use. Describing how to play the game to other children is often the biggest challenge. Sometimes games designed by children are easily understood by their peers, and sometimes they are not. Children acquire valuable feedback when other children attempt to play their games. If the game doesn't work, they must analyze why and attempt to make changes.

How can teachers assess children's mathematical knowledge as they play path games?

Teachers can readily observe children's levels of quantification and thinking strategies as they play math games. They can record observations of children's quantification, errors in thinking, and understanding of addition to share with parents and help guide planning for the classroom. Teachers may want to note these observations on index cards, in a log or journal, or on an assessment form, such as the one in the appendix.

More Path Game Activities

7.1a Walking Upside Down
Short Path

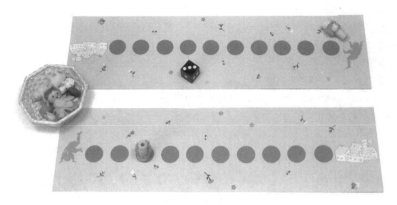

Description
The very idea of walking upside down is interesting to young children. This short path game capitalizes on that interest as children advance an upside-down mover toward the end of the path. Children often associate this game with the book *Silly Sally,* by Audrey Wood. In the book, Silly Sally walks to town backwards and upside down. The characters she meets also do silly things backwards and upside down, such as dancing and singing. Children may repeat the game by advancing additional movers—a pig, loon, and dog—along the path.

Math Concepts
▲ one-to-one correspondence
▲ quantification
▲ creation and comparison of sets

Materials
▲ 2 pieces of yellow poster board (6 by 22 inches each)
▲ twenty 1-inch purple circles, to form 2 separate paths, each with 10 spaces
▲ 2 silhouette stickers, placed upside down for the starting points
▲ 2 illustrations of a town, to form the endpoints
▲ flower stickers, to decorate the game boards
▲ 2 spool dolls, mounted upside down on a wooden disk
▲ a 1–3 die, made by adhering ¼-inch round file stickers to a 1-inch cube in sets of 1 to 3
▲ additional movers to represent the dog, loon, pig, sheep, and right-side-up characters (2 of each)

Child's Level
This game is most appropriate for children who can quantify to three and have had many experiences playing short path games with a single mover per person. The extra decorations and the additional movers add to the complexity of this short path game.

What to Look For

Some children will advance the upside-down mover along the path according to the roll of the die but disregard the additional movers.

Some children will advance all the movers along the path in a one-to-one correspondence manner.

Some children may play with the movers, which are very intriguing, but disregard the path.

Some children will place the additional movers on the path as if it were a grid.

Some children may roll the die and hop to the end of the path without regard for the quantity rolled on the die.

Modification

For younger or less experienced children, eliminate the additional movers.

Questions to Extend Thinking

How many more spaces do you need to move to get to town?
If I roll a three, will I get to the town?
Does the dog want to walk to town too?
How many characters will be in the town after they all arrive?

Integrated Curriculum Activities

Include the book *Silly Sally*, by Audrey Wood (New York: Harcourt, 1992) in the reading area.

Design other math games with upside-down characters (activities 5.14, 6.1, and 7.1b).

Add a sunbonnet with flowers for patterning to the dramatic play or manipulative area (activity 2.8). Flowers are a dominant feature of the illustrations in the book *Silly Sally*.

Create a class book using photographs of children mounted upside down with the sentence, "Silly _____ went to town, _____ backwards, upside down." Fill in the first blank with the name of the child and the second blank with the label for what the child is doing. The result might look like this: "Silly <u>Claire</u> went to town. <u>Stapling</u> backwards, upside down."

7.1b Walking Upside Down
Long Path

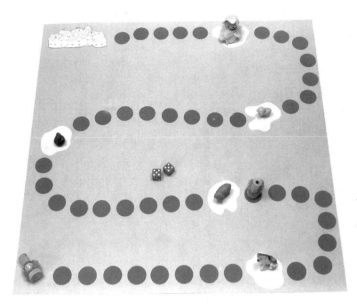

Description

Many children love to imagine acting silly, like the characters in the book *Silly Sally*, by Audrey Wood. Silly Sally walks to town backwards and upside down. Along the way she meets a dog, loon, pig, and sheep. In this math game, children use the upside-down movers to advance along the path, which includes bonus spaces with illustrations of characters from the book. Small figures representing the characters are placed on the bonus spaces. Children may collect additional movers that represent the characters as they pass each bonus space and continue to advance along the path with all the characters.

Math Concepts

▲ one-to-one correspondence
▲ creation and comparison of sets
▲ addition

Materials

▲ yellow game board (22 by 22 inches)
▲ 45 purple circles, to form the path
▲ 5 white irregular shapes, to form the bonus spaces for the characters in the book
▲ 2 silhouette stickers, placed upside down for the starting points
▲ illustration of a town, to form the endpoint
▲ 2 or 3 spool dolls, mounted upside down on wooden disks
▲ small rubber figures of a dog, loon, pig, and sheep
▲ spool doll decorated with yellow felt, to represent the right-side-up character
▲ two 1–6 dice

Child's Level

This game is most appropriate for older preschool and kindergarten children who are ready to add the quantities on a pair of regular dice. The game follows the story line of a book, has well defined bonus spaces, and includes additional movers to advance along the path. Children may need to discuss ideas for playing the game with the teacher or with each other.

What to Look For

Some children will roll two dice and add them together by counting all the dots before moving along the path.

Some children may advance each mover along the path, rather than collect them at the bonus spaces.

Some children may advance the upside-down mover along the path and ignore the characters in the bonus spaces.

Some children may roll one die and advance along the path according to the amount shown.

Modifications

Use one standard 1–6 die if the pair of dice is too difficult for the children.

Use a ten-sided die for more advanced children.

Questions to Extend Thinking

How should we play this game? What happens if I land on the space with the dog?

If I roll a seven on the dice, will I pass the loon or stop before the loon?

What happens when we land on the right-side-up character?

Integrated Curriculum Activities

Include the book *Silly Sally,* by Audrey Wood (New York: Harcourt, 1992) in the reading area.

Design other math games with upside-down characters (activities 5.14, 6.1, and 7.1a).

Assemble a shoe collection for sorting and classifying (see *More Than Counting,* activity 3.3).

Place a tray of moist sand and an assortment of small novelty shoes in the science area. Children can observe the imprints made by each type of shoe (see *More Than Magnets,* activity 2.14).

Helpful Hints

Wrap different colors of lace or ribbon around the spools of the upside-down movers.

Wrap yellow ribbon or felt around the spool of the right-side-up mover.

7.2a Baby Owls
Short Path

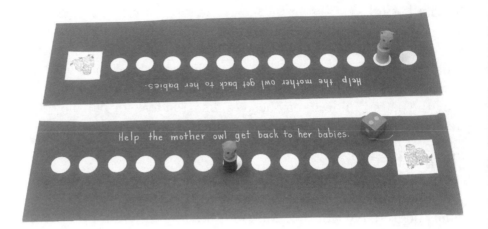

Description

Young children relate to the characters in the book *Owl Babies,* by Martin Waddell. The baby owls wait in their nest for their mother to return. Children often respond to separation from their mother by saying, "I want my mommy." In this math game, children advance a mother owl along the path to return home to her three babies.

Math Concepts

▲ one-to-one correspondence
▲ quantification
▲ creation and comparison of sets

Materials

▲ 2 pieces of black poster board (6 by 18 inches each)
▲ 24 white self-adhesive circles, to form 2 separate paths, each with 12 spaces
▲ rubber stamp imprints of 3 owls at the end of each path
▲ silver paint marker to write "Help the mother owl get back to her babies" across the top of each board
▲ 2 small owl movers
▲ a 1–3 die

Helpful Hints

Use a hot glue gun to secure the owls to a wooden spool or disk.

Child's Level
This game is most appropriate for children who can quantify to three and are just beginning to play short path games. The path is straight and clear, with no additional movers or items to collect at the end of the path.

What to Look For
Children may advance along the path according to the roll of the die.

Some children may hop to the end of the path without regard for the amount shown on the die.

Some children may roll the die, accurately quantify the amount shown, but advance too few or too many spaces along the path.

Modification
Add fill-in strips at the end of the game. Children can write their names in the blank space to complete the sentence, "I want my mommy, said _____."

Questions to Extend Thinking
How do you know how many spaces to move on the path?
If you roll a two next time, will the mother owl reach her babies?
How many more spaces before my mother owl reaches the end?

Integrated Curriculum Activities
Include the book *Owl Babies,* by Martin Waddell (Cambridge, MA: Candlewick, 1992), in the reading area.

Design other owl or bird math games (activities 5.10, 6.2, and 7.2b).

Read other owl books to the children, such as *Good-Night Owl,* by Pat Hutchins (New York: Macmillan, 1972) and *Owl: See How They Grow,* by Mary Ling (New York: Dorling Kindersley, 1992).

Introduce a flannel board activity based on characters from a story about owls (activity 8.14).

Put word cards with the names of the characters from *Owl Babies* in the writing center.

Let children dramatize owls perching on branches, flapping their wings, and flying.

7.2b Baby Owls
Long Path

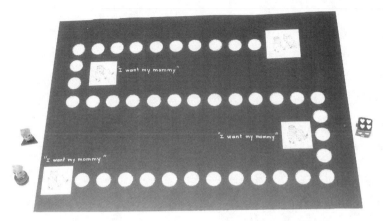

Description

This long path game coordinates well with the book *Owl Babies,* by Martin Waddell. In the story, three baby owls wait in their nest for the return of the mother owl. Throughout the story, the youngest owl, like many young children, cries, "I want my mommy." An illustration of three owls, along with the words "I want my mommy," is placed in three places on the game board. Children may determine rules or guidelines for play at each of these illustrations as they advance the mother owl mover toward the end of the path.

Math Concepts

▲ one-to-one correspondence
▲ quantification
▲ creation and comparison of sets

Materials

▲ black poster board (16 by 22 inches)
▲ 35 white 1-inch self-adhesive circles, to form the path
▲ 3 white squares, each with rubber stamp impressions of 3 owls, placed along the path as shown
▲ 1 white square, with rubber stamp impressions of 3 owls, for the endpoint
▲ silver paint marker, to print "I want my mommy" at each illustration of the 3 owls
▲ 2 owl movers, mounted on spools of different colors
▲ a 1–6 die

Child's Level

This game is most appropriate for children who can quantify to six and are just beginning to play long path games. The path is very clear because it is straight, has right angle turns instead of curves, and does not have trap or bonus spaces. While a single 1–6 die provides a challenge, it does not require children to add together the quantities on a pair of regular dice.

What to Look For

Some children will roll the die and move an equivalent number of
  spaces along the path.

Some children will roll the die and attempt to move an equivalent
  number of spaces, but skip or double-count some spaces.

Some children may hop to the end of the path without regard for
  the amount shown on the die. A grid or short path game may
  better meet their stage of development.

Modification

Use a pair of dice for children who are ready to add two dice
together.

Questions to Extend Thinking

How many spaces will you move before you reach the picture of
  the baby owls?

What do I have to roll on the die to catch up to your owl?

If you roll a four on the die, will you get home to the babies?

Integrated Curriculum Activities

Include the book *Owl Babies,* by Martin Waddell (Cambridge, MA:
  Candlewick, 1992) in the reading area.

Design other owl or bird math games (activities 5.10, 6.2, and
  7.2a).

Use owl-shaped cookie cutters as a printing tool at the easel.

Use an owl rubber stamp and 2-inch graph paper to encourage
  children to create a one-to-one relationship between the stamp
  impression and each space on the graph paper.

Helpful Hints

Small rubber owls can
be found in nature,
craft, or party supply
stores.

7.3a Pirate Treasure
Short Path

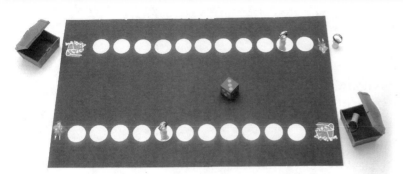

Description

Many young children like to search for and collect treasures. In this short path game, children can pretend to be pirates collecting rings for a treasure chest. Rings are used for the movers. Children may associate the game with the pirate story *Tough Boris,* by Mem Fox.

Math Concepts

▲ one-to-one correspondence
▲ quantification
▲ creation and comparison of sets

Materials

▲ black poster board (12 by 20 inches)
▲ 24 gold 1-inch circles, to form 2 separate paths, each with 12 spaces
▲ 2 pirate stickers, for the starting points
▲ 2 treasure chest stickers, for the endpoints
▲ 2 or more treasure movers, made by gluing a plastic ring onto a wooden spool
▲ a 1–3 die
▲ additional treasure movers (optional)
▲ 2 small treasure chests, to hold the treasure at the end of the path

Helpful Hints

Office supply stores carry gold seals that can be used to form the path.

Child's Level

This game is most appropriate for children who can quantify to three and have had some experience playing short path games. The additional movers create more complexity for children who may be transitioning from short to long path games. The collection of treasures encourages children to consider other mathematical relationships, such as quantification and comparison of amounts of treasure.

What to Look For

Some children will advance their movers according to the quantity rolled on the die.

Some children will repeat the process of advancing along the path in order to take more treasure to the treasure chest.

Some children may play with the treasure without regard for the game board.

Some children may place one piece of treasure on each space of the short path as if it were a grid game. They are focusing on one-to-one correspondence.

Modifications

For younger or less experienced children, eliminate the extra rings.

For older children, include paper and pencils at the end of the game. Encourage children to quantify and record the amount of treasure they collect.

Questions to Extend Thinking

How many pieces of treasure have you each collected? How do you know?

If I collect one more piece of treasure, will I have just as many pieces as you do?

Do you have enough treasure to place one on each gold space? (Use this question if a child is not advancing the mover along the path, but seems to be focusing on one-to-one correspondence with concrete objects.)

Integrated Curriculum Activities

Include the book *Tough Boris,* by Mem Fox (New York: Harcourt, 1994) in the reading area.

Design pirate grid and long path games (activity 6.3 and 7.3b).

Set up the dramatic play area as a costume shop with a variety of props, including pirate hats, for dress-up.

7.3b Pirate Treasure
Long Path

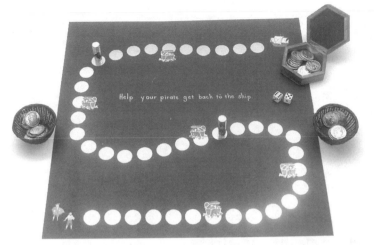

Description
Children are often fascinated with pirates and the prospect of finding treasure. This long path game coordinates well with pirate books, such as *Tough Boris,* by Mem Fox. Children advance a pirate mover along a path that sometimes crosses a treasure chest bonus space. Children can collect gold coins at each of the treasure chests.

Math Concepts
▲ one-to-one correspondence
▲ quantification
▲ creation and comparison of sets
▲ addition

Materials
▲ black poster board (22 by 22 inches)
▲ 41 gold squares, to form the path
▲ 2 pirate stickers, for the starting point
▲ 1 pirate ship sticker, for the endpoint
▲ 5 treasure chest stickers, for the bonus spaces
▲ 20 or more gold coins, to collect at the bonus spaces
▲ 2 pirate movers, made with pirate stickers secured with clear packing tape to 2 different colors of marker lids
▲ two 1–6 dice
▲ 1 basket or treasure box to hold the gold coins

Child's Level
This game is most appropriate for older preschool and kindergarten children who are interested in bonus spaces and can add together the quantities on a pair of dice. The path crosses over the treasure chest bonus spaces, thus encouraging children to consider them as part of the game, rather than decoration.

What to Look For

Some children will add the dice together by counting all the dots and advance an equivalent number of spaces along the path.

Some children may generate rules of playing the game, such as each player has to collect five gold coins.

Some children may compare quantities of gold coins they each collect.

Some children will ignore the bonus spaces.

Some children will remember some of the addition combinations after repeated experiences adding two dice.

Modifications

Change the treasure pieces from gold coins to costume jewelry. Ask kindergarten children to graph the quantities of gold and silver jewelry they collect.

Ask children to roll a die to determine how many gold coins to collect.

Use one die for children who are not yet ready to add two dice together.

Questions to Extend Thinking

What should happen if I land on the treasure chest?

How many gold coins do each of you get if you land on the treasure chest?

Do you each have the same number of gold coins?

How can you divide the gold coins so that each person has the same amount?

Integrated Curriculum Activities

Include the book *Tough Boris,* by Mem Fox (New York: Harcourt, 1994) in the reading area.

Design pirate grid and short path games (activities 6.3 and 7.3a).

Include a collection of international money for sorting and classifying (see *More Than Counting,* activity 3.10).

Helpful Hints

Look in craft and carnival supply catalogs for gold coins.

Ask parents for donations of costume jewelry to use as the treasure.

7.4a The Spider and the Fly
Short Path

Description

In this game, children roll a die and move a fly along the path until it gets caught in a spider web. The game coordinates with the book *The Very Busy Spider,* by Eric Carle, in which a "pesky" fly gets caught in a spider's web at the end of the story. The web at the end of the path is drawn with a silver paint marker.

Math Concepts

▲ one-to-one correspondence
▲ quantification
▲ creation and comparison of sets

Materials

▲ 2 pieces of green poster board (6 by 22 inches each)
▲ 20 white 1-inch self-adhesive circles, to form 2 separate paths, each with 10 spaces
▲ rubber stamp impression of a fly, to form the start points
▲ rubber stamp impression of a spider web, for the endpoints
▲ silver paint marker, to trace over the spider web
▲ 2 fly movers, made with plastic flies glued onto wooden spools
▲ a 1–3 die

Child's Level

This game is appropriate for children who are just beginning to play short path games and can quantify to three. The path is short, straight, and very clear.

What to Look For

Some children will roll the die and move an equivalent number of spaces along the path.

Some children may quantify the number of dots on the die but not move a corresponding number of spaces along the path.

Some children may hop to the end of the path without regard for the die.

Modification

For more experienced children, add additional fly movers.

Questions to Extend Thinking

How many more spaces until the fly is caught in the web?

If you roll a three on the next turn, will you get to the web?

Am I closer to the web, or are you closer to the web? How do you know?

Integrated Curriculum Activities

Include the book *The Very Busy Spider*, by Eric Carle (New York: Philomel, 1984) in the reading area.

Design other spider math games (activities 5.3, 5.4, 6.4 and 7.4b).

Put a large model of a spider and a fly in the science area so children can compare them.

Take a nature walk and look for spider webs. Spray the webs with water to make them more visible.

For children with visual impairments, design a farm game with a path they can feel (activity 8.9).

Helpful Hints

Plastic flies can be found in party supply or cake decorating stores.

7.4b The Spider and the Fly
Long Path

Description

This game coordinates with *The Very Busy Spider,* by Eric Carle, in which a spider meets many farm animals as she spins her web. As the story progresses, the web grows larger until at last the spider catches a "pesky" fly. In the game, as children advance their spider movers along the path, they may land on a special fly bonus space. Each child also has a separate collection board with pictures of all the animals in the book. When players land on a fly space, they can cover an animal on their collection board until all the farm animals have been covered.

Math Concepts

▲ one-to-one correspondence
▲ quantification
▲ creation and comparison of sets
▲ addition

Helpful Hints

Plastic spiders on rings from party stores can be cut off and mounted onto a spool. Cut the legs shorter if necessary.

Materials

▲ 1 piece of green poster board (16 by 22 inches), for the path game
▲ 2 pieces of green poster board (5 by 11 inches each), for the collection boards
▲ stickers or rubber stamps of the farm animals in the book, for the illustrations on the collection board
▲ 35 white 1-inch self-adhesive circles, to form a continuous path around the large game board
▲ rubber stamp of a fly, to create several bonus spaces on the path
▲ 2 spider movers, mounted on spools of different colors
▲ 22 white marble chips, to use as counters on the farm animal board
▲ a 1–6 die or pair of regular dice
▲ 1 basket to hold the marble chips

Child's Level

This game is most appropriate for older preschool or kindergarten children who have had experiences playing path games and generating their own rules for games. The game includes instructions for play, which may be too complex for younger children. The path does not have a start or finish; therefore, children must communicate more about how they will play the game—for example, where to start and whether a player can move backward and forward on the game board.

What to Look For

Some children will quantify dots on the dice, move a corresponding number of spaces along the path, and cover an animal on their collection board each time they land on a bonus space.

Some children will quantify the dots on the dice and move a corresponding number of spaces along the path but disregard the bonus spaces and the collection board.

Some children will communicate about how to play the game.

Some children will compare the quantities of farm animals they have each covered on their collection boards.

Modifications

Design the game in the configuration of a typical long path game if the continuous path seems too confusing.

Eliminate the two collection boards, but provide small farm animals to collect when a player lands on a fly space.

Questions to Extend Thinking

How many more animals do you have to cover on your board?

Can players move forward and backward to land on a fly space?

If I roll six on my next turn, will I land on a fly space?

Integrated Curriculum Activities

Include the book *The Very Busy Spider,* by Eric Carle (New York: Philomel, 1984) in the reading area.

Design other spider math games (activities 5.3, 5.4, 6.4, and 7.4a).

Add plastic spiders and insects to sand in the sensory table. Children can use slotted spoons to pick up the bugs.

Put a collection of plastic spiders and insects in the manipulative area for sorting and classifying.

7.5a   Colorful Mice
Short Path

Description

Children like to experiment with color mixing, just as the mice do in the book *Mouse Paint,* by Ellen Stohl Walsh. In the book, three white mice hide from a gray cat and investigate colorful pots of paint. In this game, children advance a mouse mover away from the cat at the beginning of the path and toward the paint pots.

Math Concepts

▲ one-to-one correspondence
▲ quantification
▲ creation and comparison of sets

Materials

▲ black poster board (12 by 22 inches)
▲ 22 white 1-inch self-adhesive circles, to form 2 separate paths, each with 11 spaces
▲ 2 gray cat stickers, for the start points
▲ illustrations of paint pots, for the endpoints
▲ 2 mouse movers
▲ a 1–3 die

Child's Level

This game is most appropriate for children who can quantify to three and are just beginning to play path games. The path is short, straight, and clear. There are no collection pieces or extra movers.

What to Look For

Some children may quantify the dots on the die and move an equivalent number of spaces along the path.

Some children may roll the die and advance along the path but skip over some spaces.

Some children may accurately quantify the dots on the die but not yet have a concept of moving an equivalent number of spaces along the path.

Modifications

For variety, one player could use a mouse mover and the other player could use a cat mover.

Add additional mouse movers for children who are ready.

Comments and Questions to Extend Thinking

How many spaces away from the cat have you already moved?

You are two spaces away from the paint pots. Do you have to roll a two on the die to get to the end? What should you do if you roll a three?

Integrated Curriculum Activities

Include *Mouse Paint,* by Ellen Stohl Walsh (New York: Harcourt, 1989) in the reading area.

Design other mouse games for the math area (activities 6.5 and 7.5b).

Plan a foot-printing art activity.

Let children mix colors as a special activity. Water colored with food coloring or watercolor paints can be combined to create new colors.

Use spray bottles filled with food coloring and water to spray large sheets of paper in the outdoor area. Children can observe the mixing of colors.

Helpful Hints

The paint pot illustrations can be made with small rectangles of white paper. Color part of the white rectangles with a marker to look like paint inside the pot.

7.5b Colorful Mice
Long Path

Description

This game coordinates well with the book *Mouse Paint*, by Ellen Stohl Walsh. Children begin with a set of twelve marble chips, two each of red, yellow, blue, green, orange, and purple. They advance their mouse movers along a path of white dots, which also includes trap spaces made with color dots. If they land on a color dot, they lose a marble chip of that color. The object is to finish the game with the most marble chips. Some children may wish to generate additional rules for play.

Math Concepts

▲ one-to-one correspondence
▲ quantification
▲ creation and comparison of sets
▲ addition and subtraction

Materials

▲ black poster board (22 by 22 inches)
▲ 50 white 1-inch self-adhesive circles
▲ red, yellow, blue, green, orange, and purple markers, to color the bonus spaces
▲ 2 white mouse movers, mounted on a silver and gold spool
▲ two 1–6 dice, or one 10-sided die

Child's Level

This game is most appropriate for kindergarten children, since it involves following a set of directions and keeping track of how many marble chips are left. The use of a pair of 1–6 dice or a 10-sided die also increases the complexity of the game.

What to Look For

Some children will add two dice together by counting all the dots, move an equivalent number of spaces along the path, keep track of how many marble chips they have left, and accurately compare sets of marble chips at the end of the game.

Some children may not want to use the trap spaces as described. They may wish to collect marble chips rather than lose them!

Some children may advance along the path and follow the guidelines, but may not be able to compare the quantities of marble chips they each have.

Modifications

Three or more children could play the game. Several children could have mouse movers and one could have a cat mover. The cat could try to catch the mice and take away the marble chips.

For a simpler version of the game, the guidelines for play can be eliminated and children can decide what happens if a player lands on a color dot.

Questions to Extend Thinking

How do you know that you each began with the same number of marble chips?

How many fewer marble chips do you have than I have?

What do you have to roll in order to avoid the trap space?

Integrated Curriculum Activities

Include *Mouse Paint,* by Ellen Stohl Walsh (New York: Harcourt, 1989) in the reading area.

Design other mouse games for the math area (activities 6.5 and 7.5a).

Plan a graphing activity in which each child is given 1-inch graph paper and varying amounts of ¾-inch self-adhesive dots in a variety of colors. Children can graph the dots by color and tally the totals for each color. The teacher will have a permanent record of each child's ability to graph and to quantify.

Introduce the game at group or circle time so you can suggest guidelines for play or allow children to generate rules for play.

7.6a Tumbling Alphabet
Short Path

Description
Many children quickly memorize the rhyming text of the alphabet book *Chicka Chicka Boom Boom,* by Bill Martin, Jr., and John Archambault. This short path game coordinates with the book. Children advance one or more alphabet letters along a path to a coconut tree, just as the poem in the book suggests.

Math Concepts
▲ one-to-one correspondence
▲ quantification
▲ creation and comparison of sets

Materials
▲ white poster board (16 by 22 inches), with a 1-inch border made of fluorescent pink poster board and orange dots
▲ twenty 1-inch fluorescent pink circles, to form 2 separate paths, each with 10 spaces
▲ 2 palm tree stickers, for the endpoints
▲ 2 or more movers, made by gluing alphabet erasers onto wooden spools
▲ a 1–3 die

Helpful Hints
Use super glue to attach the erasers to the spool. Hot glue does not permanently adhere erasers to the wooden spools.

Child's Level
This game is most appropriate for children who can quantify to three and have had some experience playing short path games. The design of the game board includes extra decoration, which could be confusing to children who have never played a short path game. The inclusion of more than one mover to advance along the path adds more complexity to the game. The path is short enough to encourage children to repeat the game using the additional alphabet movers.

What to Look For

Some children will roll the die and advance an equivalent number of spaces along the path.

Some children may advance one mover to the end of the path and then return to the beginning to advance a second or third mover to the end.

Some children may focus on the letters on the movers and disregard the mathematical component of the game.

Modification

For variety, use Duplo people as the movers and have children collect letters at the end of the game. Some children will want to collect the letters in their name.

Comments and Questions to Extend Thinking

How many more spaces do you have to move until you reach the coconut tree?

You are closer to the coconut tree than I am. How many more spaces do I have to move to be just as close as you are?

How many letters do you have in your coconut tree?

Integrated Curriculum Activities

Include *Chicka Chicka Boom Boom,* by Bill Martin, Jr., and John Archambault (New York: Simon, 1989) in the reading area.

Design other alphabet math games (activities 6.6 and 7.6b).

Plan a gluing activity using alphabet pasta.

Make gelatin in the shape of alphabet letters.

Display coconuts in the science area. Children can guess what's inside before opening the coconuts (see *More Than Magnets,* activity 2.10).

Use hollow coconut shells as rhythm instruments (see *More Than Singing,* activity 4.8).

7.6b Tumbling Alphabet
Long Path

Description

Preschool and kindergarten children sometimes use a movable alphabet, such as wooden or plastic letters, to form their names and other high-interest words. This long path game provides opportunities for children to collect letters when they reach the coconut tree at the end of the path. Children advance people movers to the coconut tree, collect alphabet letters, and match the letters to word cards. This game can be used in conjunction with the alphabet book *Chicka Chicka Boom Boom,* by Bill Martin, Jr., and John Archambault.

Math Concepts

▲ one-to-one correspondence
▲ quantification
▲ addition
▲ creation and comparison of sets

Materials

▲ white poster board (22 by 22 inches), with a 1-inch border made from fluorescent pink poster board and orange dots
▲ 45 press-on alphabet letters or other precut alphabet letters, placed in random order to form the path
▲ 2 or more people movers, such as Fisher-Price or Duplo people
▲ several sets of wooden or plastic alphabet letters, or alphabet erasers
▲ basket or other container for the alphabet letters
▲ two 1–6 dice
▲ word cards, made by tracing around the letters used in the game or with alphabet rubber stamps (optional)

Child's Level

This game is most appropriate for older preschool and kindergarten children. Younger children may focus on the letters rather than on the mathematical components of the game. If the optional word cards are included, the teacher should begin with the names of the children. Later, other high-interest words can be added.

What to Look For

Some children will roll the dice, add the quantities together, and move an equivalent number of spaces along the path.

Some children will accurately quantify the dice but make errors as they advance along the path, such as re-counting the space they occupy or skipping spaces.

Some children may be curious about the random sequencing of the alphabet letters that form the path.

Some children may use the alphabet letters to spell words, without using the math game.

Modifications

If children primarily focus on the letters, use 1-inch circles instead of alphabet letters to form the path. Children can collect letters at the end of the game.

For variety, replace some of the alphabet letters on the path with fluorescent pink circles to use as bonus spaces. When children land on the bonus space, they can collect an alphabet letter from the coconut tree.

Comments and Questions to Extend Thinking

How many letters do each of you collect when you reach the coconut tree?

You are getting close to the coconut tree. Can you roll the exact quantity you need if you use only one die?

Integrated Curriculum Activities

Include *Chicka Chicka Boom Boom,* by Bill Martin, Jr., and John Archambault (New York: Simon, 1989) in the reading area.

Design other alphabet math games (activities 6.6 and 7.6a).

Sing songs that focus on letters, such as a version of bingo that incorporates the children's names (see *More Than Singing,* activity 2.11).

Include alphabet rubber stamps at the writing center.

Helpful Hints

Small alphabet blocks can be substituted for the sets of alphabet letters.

7.7a Grandma's Cookies
Short Path

Description

This short path game coordinates well with the book *The Doorbell Rang*, by Pat Hutchins. Children use people movers to advance along a path toward a cookie sheet filled with cookies. In the book, children share chocolate chip cookies among themselves.

Math Concepts

▲ one-to-one correspondence
▲ quantification
▲ creation and comparison of sets

Materials

▲ 2 pieces of brown poster board (6 by 22 inches each)
▲ 24 white 1-inch self-adhesive circles, to form 2 separate paths, each with 12 spaces
▲ 2 silhouette stickers, for the start points
▲ 2 cookie sheet stickers, for the endpoints
▲ 2 people movers, such as Duplo or Fisher-Price people
▲ a 1–3 die

Child's Level

This game is most appropriate for children who can quantify to three and are just beginning to play short path games. The path is short, straight, and very clear.

What to Look For

Some children may roll the die and move an equivalent number of
spaces along the path.

Some children may accurately quantify the number of dots on the
die but not be able to move an equivalent number of spaces
along the path.

Some children may play with the people in a pretend play manner.

Modifications

Add collection pieces, such as plastic cookies, at the end of the
path. Each time a child reaches the cookie sheet, she collects a
cookie.

Provide more people as movers, so that children can repeat the
game.

Comments and Questions to Extend Thinking

How many more spaces do you have to move until you reach the
cookies?

I rolled three on the die. I'm going to move three—one, two, three.
(Use this comment if the child ignores the die.)

If you roll two on the die, will you get to the cookies?

Integrated Curriculum Activities

Include *The Doorbell Rang,* by Pat Hutchins (New York: Greenwillow, 1986) in the reading area.

Design other cookie games for the math area (activities 6.7 and
7.7b).

Set up a bakery in the dramatic play area (activity 1.1).

Sing a counting song about cookies (activity 5.6).

Let children vote on their favorite type of cookie and graph the
results.

Helpful Hints

So children don't take
the people movers from
the game and use them
in the manipulative
area, use different
kinds of people figures
in the two areas.

7.7b Grandma's Cookies
Long Path

Description

Kindergarten children often explore the concept of division during the daily activities of school. They might divide the pretzels for snack or the markers used for art. In this long path game, children may consider the division of cookies after they advance along the path and collect cookies at the bonus spaces. This game coordinates with the book *The Doorbell Rang,* by Pat Hutchins, in which children must solve the problem of how to divide the cookies each time more children join the group.

Math Concepts

▲ one-to-one correspondence
▲ quantification
▲ creation and comparison of sets
▲ addition, subtraction, and division

Materials

▲ brown poster board (22 by 22 inches)
▲ 50 white 1-inch self-adhesive circles
▲ rubber stamp of a cookie, to make the bonus spaces
▲ plastic cookies to collect
▲ 2 or more people movers, such as Duplo or Fisher-Price
▲ two 1–6 dice
▲ 1 basket or cookie jar for the endpoint, to hold the cookies
▲ 1 small basket or tray for each child, to store the cookies collected
▲ paper and pencils, for recording and computation (optional)

Child's Level

This game is most appropriate for kindergarten children who can quantify using a pair of regular dice and have played games with guidelines for play. The bonus spaces and the inclusion of two 1–6 dice make this game too complex for younger or less experienced children. The teacher may need to discuss the game with children before it is available for use. Children may generate additional or different guidelines for how to play this game.

What to Look For

Some children will add the dice together by counting all the dots, move an equivalent number of spaces along the path, collect cookies at the bonus spaces, and compare how many cookies each player has collected at the end of the game.

Some children may ignore the bonus spaces and collect cookies at the end of the game.

Some children may place one cookie on top of each bonus space.

Some children will generate rules for playing the game.

Some children will associate the game with the book and attempt to collect cookies and divide them.

Modifications

Use three dice for children who are ready to add more quantities together.

To focus on subtraction, let each child begin the game with twelve cookies. If a child lands on a cookie space, they must give up one cookie. The object is to try to get to the cookie jar with the most cookies.

Questions to Extend Thinking

How many cookies have you each collected?

If you divide the cookies, how many will you each have?

What do you have to roll to collect a cookie?

Integrated Curriculum Activities

Include *The Doorbell Rang,* by Pat Hutchins (New York: Greenwillow, 1986) in the reading area.

Design other cookie games for the math area (activities 6.7 and 7.7a).

Read other baking books, such as *Jake Baked a Cake,* by B. G. Hennessy (New York: Viking, 1990) and *Mister Cookie Baker,* by Monica Wellington (New York: Dutton, 1992).

Helpful Hints

Cookie magnets can be found in many grocery or kitchen supply stores.

7.8a Construction Zone
Short Path

Description

This short path game can be used when construction or repair work occurs near the school. It coordinates well with a dramatic play area set up like a construction site, with hard hats, work gloves, and pretend tools. Children are typically intrigued by real tools, such as hammers, saws, and screwdrivers. In this game, people movers carry tools to a tool chest.

Math Concepts

▲ one-to-one correspondence
▲ quantification
▲ creation and comparison of sets

Materials

▲ 2 pieces of dark blue poster board (6 by 22 inches each)
▲ 20 yellow 1-inch circles or squares, to form 2 separate paths, each with 10 spaces
▲ 2 silhouette stickers, for the starting points
▲ 2 tool chest stickers, for the endpoints
▲ ½-inch-wide yellow tape, to form the border around the game boards
▲ 2 plastic people, each with magnetic tape on the front
▲ small plastic tools, with magnetic tape attached
▲ a 1–3 die
▲ 2 small baskets for the tools

Child's Level

This game is most appropriate for preschool and kindergarten children who can quantify to three and have had some experience playing short path games. The additional tools to take to the tool chest add complexity to the game.

What to Look For

Some children will roll the die and move an equivalent number of spaces on the path.

Some children will return to the beginning of the path to take additional tools to the tool chest.

Some children may place each of the tools on one space of the path. They are thinking about one-to-one correspondence in a way that is similar to grid games.

Modification

For a simpler version of the game, eliminate the additional tools to take to the tool chest.

Questions to Extend Thinking

How many tools do you have to take to the tool chest?

Do we each have the same number of tools? How do you know?

How can we divide the tools so that we each have the same amount to begin the game?

Integrated Curriculum Activities

Design other construction games for the math area (activities 6.8 and 7.8b).

Read construction books, such as *Bam Bam Bam*, by Eve Merriam (New York: Scholastic, 1994), *Machines At Work*, by Byron Barton (New York: Harper, 1987), and *Skyscraper Going Up*, by Vicki Cobb (New York: Crowell, 1987).

Put word cards with the names of tools or types of trucks in the writing area.

Add trucks to the block area.

Helpful Hints

Small plastic tools can sometimes be found in party and carnival supply catalogs. As a substitute for plastic tools, laminate tool stickers and attach magnetic tape.

7.8b Construction Zone
Long Path

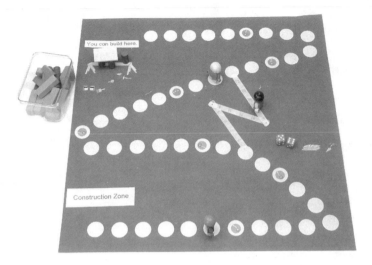

Description

Children love to dress up as construction workers and pretend to build things. This game builds on that interest and coordinates with books related to construction, such as *Machines at Work,* by Byron Barton, or *The Tool Box,* by Anne and Harlow Rockwell. In this long path game, children advance along a path that contains trap and bonus spaces. The object is to use a collection of small blocks to build a structure at the end of the path. Although children work independently to reach the endpoint, they work cooperatively to construct a structure with the blocks.

Math Concepts

▲ one-to-one correspondence
▲ quantification
▲ creation and comparison of sets
▲ addition and subtraction

Materials

▲ dark blue poster board (22 by 22 inches)
▲ 45 yellow 1-inch circles or squares
▲ illustration of yellow measuring tape, for the shortcut, as shown above
▲ tape measure stickers, to form the trap spaces
▲ 2 or more people movers
▲ basket of small, wooden table blocks
▲ two 1–6 dice, or one 10-sided die

Child's Level

This game is most appropriate for kindergarten children who can quantify using a pair of regular dice and who have had some experience playing less complex long path games. The trap and bonus spaces may be too confusing for younger, less experienced children. The need to cooperate to construct a structure is appealing to many kindergarten children.

What to Look For

Some children may roll the dice, move an equivalent number of spaces, follow the directions on the trap and bonus spaces, and cooperate to build a structure with the blocks at the end of the game.

Some children may roll the dice, move an equivalent number of spaces, follow the trap and bonus directions, but choose not to use the blocks at the end for building.

Some children may generate different guidelines for playing the game. Kindergarten children often make up more complex rules.

Some children may accurately quantify the dots on the die but make errors as they advance along the path, such as double-counting or skipping a space. They may also make addition errors.

Modifications

Suggest that children collect a block at each of the tape measure stickers.

Add a third die for children who are ready to add three quantities together.

Questions to Extend Thinking

What should happen if I land on a tape measure?

What do you have to roll to avoid the tape measure trap?

Is it possible to reach the end of the game if you roll the pair of dice?

Integrated Curriculum Activities

Design other construction games for the math area (activities 6.8 and 7.8a).

Read construction books, such as *Machines At Work*, by Byron Barton (New York: Harper, 1987), *The Tool Box*, by Anne and Harlow Rockwell (New York: Macmillan, 1971), and *Changes, Changes*, by Pat Hutchins (New York: Macmillan, 1971).

Put small colored blocks in the block area as additional props for building.

Use a paper tape measure for the short-cut. Hardware stores sometimes distribute them as advertisements.

7.9a Taking Care of Baby
Short Path

Description

Young children are often fascinated with babies and toddlers. They feel grown up enough to help care for them. This short path game gives children an opportunity to take baby items along a path to a baby. Since early childhood classrooms typically include a dramatic play area with dolls to care for, this game coordinates with activities in that area.

Math Concepts

▲ one-to-one correspondence
▲ quantification
▲ creation and comparison of sets

Materials

▲ light blue or other pastel-colored poster board (12 by 22 inches)
▲ 22 white 1-inch self-adhesive circles, to form 2 separate paths, each with 11 spaces
▲ several baby items, such as bottles, rattles, teddy bears, and pacifiers, to use as movers
▲ 2 small baskets, to collect the baby items at the end of the game
▲ a 1–3 die

Child's Level

This game is most appropriate for preschool or kindergarten children who can quantify to three and have had some experience playing short path games using one mover per person.

What to Look For

Some children will roll the die and move an equivalent number of spaces along the path. After reaching the end, they may repeat the process to take additional items to the baby.

Some children may take one baby item to the end of the path and ignore the additional movers.

Some children may compare the quantities of baby items they each have.

Some children may place one baby item on each space of the path. They are thinking about one-to-one correspondence in a way that is similar to a grid game.

Some children may quantify the number of baby items but ignore the path.

Modifications

For a simpler version of the game, begin with one mover for each player. More movers can be added after a week or more of play.

For variety, change the movers to toy people and collect things for the baby at the end of the path.

Questions to Extend Thinking

How many things will you take to the baby?

Do we each have the same amount of bottles for the babies?

If I take one more item to my baby, will my baby have just as many things as yours?

Integrated Curriculum Activities

Design other baby games for the math area (activities 6.9 and 7.9b).

Set up the dramatic play area with props needed to care for babies, such as bottles, diapers, rattles, and blankets.

Wash dolls in the sensory table.

Invite a parent with a baby to visit the classroom and bathe the baby while the children watch.

Use chalk or paint to draw a path in the outside area. Children can roll a large die and push baby strollers along the path (activity 1.16).

7.9b Taking Care of Baby
Long Path

Description
Young children enjoy collecting things. They can spend a long period of time assembling rocks, leaves, or even twigs. This baby game gives children the opportunity to collect small baby items. The path does not have a beginning or end; children may start at any point on the path. The path includes gold spaces with the words "Take a card." When players land on one of the spaces, they take a card to find out what to collect for baby. The items are stored in small plastic baskets or cradles.

Thanks to Dena Papin for this game.

Math Concepts
▲ one-to-one correspondence
▲ quantification
▲ creation and comparison of sets
▲ addition

Materials
▲ light blue or other pastel-colored poster board (22 by 22 inches)
▲ 17 white paper ovals, cut to fit the size of the mover
▲ 6 or more gold ovals, the same size as the white ones
▲ 2 small cradles for movers, one pink and one blue
▲ collection of baby items, such as bottles, rattles, diaper pins, pacifiers, and teddy bears
▲ set of cards, with stickers or illustrations of the collection items
▲ 2 small baskets, one for the cards and one for the baby items
▲ a 1–6 die

Child's Level
This game is most appropriate for preschool and kindergarten children who can quantify to six and have had some experience playing long path games.

What to Look For

Some children will quantify the dots on the die, move an equivalent number of spaces along the path, and collect a baby item each time they land on a bonus space.

Some children may choose to go both forward and backward in order to land on a gold space.

Some children may compare their quantities of baby items at the end of the game.

Some children may fix the die so that they will land on a gold space on the next turn. They can mentally count the quantity of spaces before the gold space and can match that amount on the die.

Modifications

Ask kindergarten children to graph the results of the baby items they collect. This will give you a permanent record for assessment.

Suggest that children use a 1–3 die to determine how many of each item they should collect when they draw a card.

Questions to Extend Thinking

Do you have just as many bottles for your baby as you have rattles?

How many more teddy bears do you need to collect for the baby so that you have just as many bears as pacifiers?

How many things will your baby have if you collect one of each item?

Integrated Curriculum Activities

Design other baby games for the math area (activities 6.9 and 7.9a).

Set up the dramatic play area with props needed to care for babies, such as bottles, diapers, rattles, and blankets.

Sing baby songs (see *More Than Singing,* activities 2.1, 2.9, 2.12, and 2.13).

Read books about babies, such as *Hush!* by Minfong Ho (New York: Orchard, 1996) and *Sleep, Sleep, Sleep,* by Nancy Van Laan (Boston: Little, Brown, 1995).

7.10a Let's Go Shopping
Short Path

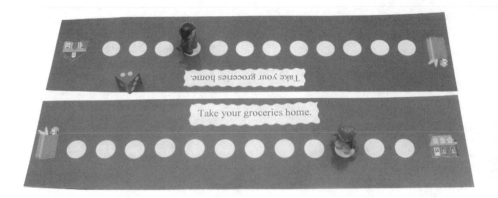

Description

Most young children have been grocery shopping with their parents. They may have had the opportunity to choose some of the food that is purchased. Many preschool and kindergarten classrooms set up a grocery store in the dramatic play area. This short path game suggests that children take groceries home from the grocery store.

Math Concepts

▲ one-to-one correspondence
▲ quantification
▲ creation and comparison of sets

Materials

▲ 2 pieces of dark blue poster board (6 by 22 inches each)
▲ 24 white 1-inch circles (1 by 1½ inches), to form 2 separate paths, each with 12 spaces
▲ 2 grocery bag stickers, for the starting points
▲ 2 house stickers, for the end points
▲ 2 people movers
▲ a 1–3 die

Helpful Hints

Use a photograph of a house or apartment building if stickers are not available.

Child's Level

This game is most appropriate for preschool or kindergarten children who can quantify to three and are just beginning to play short path games.

What to Look For

Some children will roll the die and move an equivalent number of spaces along the path.

Some children may accurately quantify the number of dots on the die but may not be able to move an equivalent number of spaces along the path.

Some children may hop the mover to the end of the path without regard for the die.

Modification

Provide additional people movers or small food items for children to collect to encourage children to repeat the game.

Questions to Extend Thinking

How many more spaces do you have to move before you reach your house?

If you roll a three on the die, will you get to your house?

Integrated Curriculum Activities

Design other grocery store games for the math area (activities 5.12, 6.10, and 7.10b).

Set up the dramatic play area as a grocery store.

Plan a field trip to a local grocery store to purchase food for a cooking activity.

7.10b Let's Go Shopping
Long Path

Description

In this long path game, children advance along a path and try to collect groceries to place in a small brown bag at the end of the path. Although children play the game independently, they collect all the groceries in one bag. At the end of the game, the children can make a list of the items collected at points along the path.

Math Concepts

▲ one-to-one correspondence
▲ quantification
▲ creation and comparison of sets
▲ addition

Materials

▲ dark blue poster board (22 by 22 inches)
▲ 48 white 1-inch self-adhesive circles, to form the path
▲ 2 silhouette stickers, for the start point
▲ 4 or 5 red squares, to form the bonus spaces
▲ collection of small groceries, such as fruits, vegetables, and tiny cans or boxes, placed in tiny baskets on the bonus spaces
▲ 1 small brown paper bag, for the end of the path
▲ 2 people movers
▲ two 1–6 dice

Child's Level

This game is most appropriate for older preschool or kindergarten children who can quantify using a pair of dice. Cooperating to collect the groceries in one bag and keeping a record of the items collected may be too difficult for younger children.

What to Look For

Some children may roll the dice, add the quantities of dots
    together, advance an equivalent number of spaces along the
    path, and collect grocery items when they land on the bonus
    spaces.

Some children may advance along the path but disregard the
    grocery items.

Some children may place all the groceries in the bag before the
    game begins and ignore the bonus spaces along the path.

Some children may divide the groceries before the play begins.

Modifications

Provide two small grocery bags so that children can collect items
    in individual bags.

For an easier version of the game, eliminate the grocery items to
    collect. The end point can be an illustration of a house or apart-
    ment building instead of the paper bag.

Questions to Extend Thinking

How many more spaces do you need to move before you can
    collect some groceries?

If you roll eight on the dice, will you go past the bonus space or
    stop before it?

How many groceries have you collected altogether?

Integrated Curriculum Activities

Design other grocery store games for the math area (activities 5.12,
    6.10, and 7.10a).

Include books about grocery stores, such as *The Supermarket,* by
    Anne and Harlow Rockwell (New York: Macmillan, 1979) and
    Feast for Ten, by Cathryn Falwell (New York: Clarion, 1993), in
    the reading area.

Take a field trip to a grocery store. Children can dictate stories
    based on the experience.

Helpful Hints

Party supply stores sell
tiny brown bags, which
can be cut with pinking
shears across the top to
look like grocery bags.

7.11a Quilt Squares
Short Path

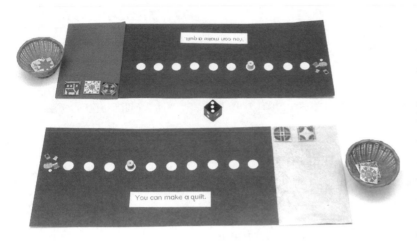

Description

Quilting is an early-American tradition teachers may wish to explore with children. They love to use large plastic needles and yarn to sew on burlap squares. These squares can be sewn together to make a quilt. This short path game allows children to create a tiny quilt on a piece of felt at the end of the path. Small quilt squares are available to place onto the felt each time a player reaches the end of the path. Children are motivated to make repeat trips along the path in order to collect more pieces to add to the quilt.

Math Concepts

▲ one-to-one correspondence
▲ quantification
▲ creation and comparison of sets
▲ patterns and symmetry

Materials

▲ 2 pieces of black poster board (8 by 22 inches each)
▲ twenty ¾-inch yellow self-adhesive circles, to form 2 separate paths, each with 10 spaces
▲ 2 tiny spools of thread, for the movers
▲ 2 pieces of colored felt (5 by 8 inches), glued to the last section of the path
▲ 18 quilt pieces (9 for each player), made from stickers or quilt rubber stamps, with Velcro attached to the back
▲ small baskets to hold the quilt pieces
▲ a 1–3 die

Child's Level

This short path game is most appropriate for older preschool and kindergarten children who can quantify to three and who have had many experiences playing short path games. The path is only ten spaces in length to encourage children to repeat the game, but the game is more complex than many other short path games.

What to Look For

Some children will quantify the number of dots on the die and move an equivalent number of spaces along the path.

Some children may roll the die and advance to the end of the path once, but complete the quilt on the first time across.

Some children may repeat the game several times in order to collect one piece for the quilt each time.

Some children may create a quilt using the felt board and quilt pieces without regard for the die.

Modification

If the game is too difficult for children, eliminate the felt board. Children can advance along the path to an illustration of a quilt cut from a catalog or calendar.

Questions to Extend Thinking

How many pieces have you collected for your quilt?

Do we each have the same number of pieces for the quilt?

What do I have to roll on the die in order to collect a quilt piece?

How many more spaces do you need to move to reach the quilt?

Integrated Curriculum Activities

Include *The Quilt*, by Ann Jonas (New York: Greenwillow, 1984), *Luka's Quilt*, by Georgia Guback (New York: Greenwillow, 1994), and *The Quilt Story*, by Tony Johnston (New York: Scholastic, 1985) in the reading area.

Design other quilt games for the math area (activities 6.11 and 7.11b).

Plan sewing activities so children can create quilt squares.

Let children create class quilts (see *More Than Painting*, activities 7.5, 7.6, 7.7, and 7.16).

7.11b Quilt Squares
Long Path

Description

This more-complex quilt game is similar to the short path quilt game (activity 7.11a), but it includes trap spaces with directions for how to play the game. The trap spaces are made with a sticker of a pair of scissors and the words "Snip Snip" written next to them. Each child has a spool mover with a removable quilt piece on top. When players reach the end of the path, they can remove the quilt piece from their spool and add it to a piece of felt to form a quilt. In this version, children cooperate to create one quilt; in the short path game, each child creates an individual quilt.

Math Concepts

▲ one-to-one correspondence
▲ quantification
▲ creation and comparison of sets
▲ patterning and symmetry

Materials

▲ black poster board (22 by 22 inches)
▲ 1 piece of colored felt (8 by 5 inches), glued to the poster board
▲ 50 white 1-inch self-adhesive circles, to form the path
▲ 5 or more scissors stickers, to form the trap spaces
▲ 15 or more small quilt pieces, made from 1-inch-square quilt stickers mounted on index cards and laminated, with Velcro attached to the back
▲ 2 spools of different colors, with Velcro attached to the top
▲ two 1–6 dice

Child's Level

This game is most appropriate for kindergarten children who have had experience playing less-complex path games and are ready to quantify by adding together the dots on a pair of dice.

What to Look For

Some children will add the two dice together by counting all the dots and then advance an equivalent number of spaces along the path.

Some children will quantify one die and move accordingly, and then quantify the second die and move accordingly. They do not yet understand the concept of adding two sets together.

Some children may make addition errors as they add the quantities on the two dice.

Some children will remember some of the addition combinations after repeated experiences adding two dice together.

Some children may create a quilt without advancing along the path.

Some children may ignore the trap spaces and continue to advance along the path.

Some children may cooperate to generate additional rules for play.

Modifications

To simplify the game, eliminate the trap spaces.

Children can use 2-inch graph paper and quilt-square rubber stamps to create the quilt at the end of the game.

For a different quantification challenge, use a ten-sided die in place of the pair of dice.

Questions to Extend Thinking

What will you need to roll on the dice in order to avoid the next trap space?

If you roll ten on the dice, will you reach the end of the path?

How many quilt pieces do you need to complete your quilt?

What kind of pattern will you create on your quilt?

Integrated Curriculum Activities

Include books about quilting, such as *Sweet Clara and the Keeping Quilt,* by Deborah Hopkinson (New York: Knopf, 1993) and *The Keeping Quilt,* by Patricia Polacco (New York: Simon, 1988), in the reading area.

Design other quilt-related math games (activities 6.11 and 7.11a).

Plan sewing activities so children can create quilt squares.

Cut shapes out of colored felt. Children can assemble them on a flannel board to create quilt designs.

Wrapping paper with quilt designs can be cut apart to replace the quilt stickers if they are not available.

Laminate the game board before gluing the felt square to it.

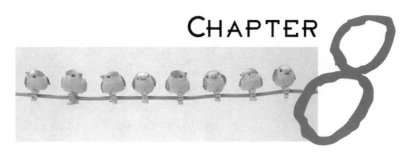

CHAPTER 8

Math for Inclusive Classrooms

Audrey sat down at the math game table and began exploring the items on the table with her hands. She located a basket of movers and carefully felt each animal before deciding on a fuzzy sheep.

Her teacher sat down at the table and asked, "Which animal can I use for the game?"

Audrey felt in the basket and handed the teacher a cow. Next Audrey began to feel the game board with her hands. She located three paths: one with Velcro squares, one with felt triangles, and one with raised metallic circles. Audrey put her sheep on the path with circles.

By this time, Bryant had arrived at the game table.

"I want to be the pig," he said.

"Which path will you use?" asked the teacher.

"The red one," Bryant replied, and pointed to the path with red Velcro squares.

Audrey found the die and rolled it. She touched the three raised stickers on the die and then moved her sheep three spaces along the path.

Bryant rolled the die and said, "Two."

Audrey, Bryant, and the teacher took turns moving their animals until they had all arrived at the end of the path, a plastic fence glued to the game board.

"We won!" Bryant shouted.

▲ ▲ ▲

Children with disabilities enjoy and benefit from the same curriculum materials as typically developing children. Simple modifications can make specific activities accessible to all children. The key is to design the materials so that they meet the needs of children with disabilities but are equally appealing to all of the children in the class. This ensures that all children can interact with one another as they utilize the materials.

Teachers' Questions

What is meant by inclusive classrooms?

*The term **inclusive classrooms** refers to programs that include children with specific disabilities as full participants in classrooms of primarily typically developing children.* Although some modifications in materials or in the classroom environment may be needed to accommodate the needs of some children with disabilities, they participate as completely as possible in all classroom activities. Support personnel, such as physical therapists or speech therapists, often work with individual children in the classroom rather than removing them for services. Children with disabilities usually have IEPs (individualized educational plans) with specific goals for their development.

Do math materials need to be changed for children with disabilities?

Sometimes. Depending on the nature of the child's disability, as well as the developmental needs of the individual child, certain math materials may need to be modified to best meet the child's needs. In many cases, however, teachers find that math materials don't need to be changed at all. This is because well-designed math activities are open-ended and accommodate a wide range of developmental levels. When math games are made in sets of increasing difficulty, an even broader spectrum of children can be challenged. For this reason, we often recommend that teachers create grid, short path, and long path games centered around the same topic. In this way, children on many different thinking levels can successfully explore math materials related to a favorite book or theme. Chapters 6 and 7 show many examples of these three types of games developed around a common topic.

What factors should teachers consider when modifying math materials for children with disabilities?

Teachers should consider the specific challenges of each child and how they may affect the child's ability to utilize each material in the classroom. The amount and type of modification needed varies dramatically depending on the individual child and the nature of the disability. For example, children with physical disabilities or impaired motor function may need larger game pieces or a game board taped to the table. While this simple change does not affect typically developing children's interest in the game or ability to use it, it is crucial to the successful participation of the child with motor challenges.

When modifying math activities, teachers should remember to keep the materials attractive and interesting for all children so that children with disabilities are not isolated when experimenting with math activities. For example, a child with a visual impairment may need raised spaces on a path game in order to tell where to move the game piece. How the game board looks may be irrelevant. On the other hand, other children may be attracted to the game because it *looks* attractive or exciting. Teachers who consider all of these needs when designing math materials foster social and cognitive interactions among children who have disabilities and children who do not.

Several activities in this chapter are modifications of activities described elsewhere in this book. They serve as examples of specific ways to modify existing materials to meet the individual needs of children with disabilities.

How can teachers encourage typically developing children to interact with children with disabilities when using math materials?

Teachers can design math materials that appeal to typically developing children as well as children with disabilities. Teachers can scaffold, or enhance, play opportunities by facilitating communication and play strategies among diverse children. Since children initially tend to notice differences among themselves—and a disability could be a notable difference—teachers can instead draw children's attention to their similarities, such as a common interest in a particular toy or activity. For example, the teacher might comment, "Mark, I noticed you and Steven both love the book *The Lady with the Alligator Purse.* Steven and I were just about to play the alligator path game. Do you want to choose an alligator mover and play with us?" At other times the teacher might help children resolve differences that arise when children of different cognitive levels try to play a game together. The teacher might say, "Latoya, I think Mary just wants to have her mover hop around when it's her turn. Maybe you and I can roll the dice for our turns, and Mary can play the way she wants to for her turn."

How might cognitive delays affect a child's use of math materials?

Children with cognitive delays may be moving through developmental stages at a slower rate than typically developing children. Thus, they may need materials designed for younger children and may also require more time to explore certain materials or concepts. Teachers may notice that children with cognitive delays quantify materials globally for a longer period of time than typically developing children and need more opportunities to explore one-to-one correspondence relationships. They may also continue to explore materials sensorially, such as by putting things into their mouths, longer than children who do not have delays. Teachers need to make note of these developmental needs when planning materials for the classroom.

How can teachers design math materials to meet the needs of children with cognitive delays?

Teachers can create simple, concrete math manipulatives, simplify existing math games, and substitute larger dice and manipulative pieces for children who still put objects into their mouths. Most preschool classrooms have children that span a range of ages and developmental levels, so skillful teachers are accustomed to planning for children at various developmental stages. When preparing math activities for children with cognitive delays, teachers may rely on some of the materials and activities suggested for younger children. Teachers can simplify existing math games by switching to a die or spinner with smaller quantities and reducing the number of manipulative pieces. Many of the math activities included in this book have suggestions for simplifying them. Teachers may also find that dice with large dots make it easier for children to explore one-to-one correspondence since they can actually place manipulative pieces on the dots. Activities 8.1 through 8.5 are specifically designed for children with cognitive delays.

How might a visual impairment affect a child's use of math materials?

Children with visual impairments range from those with significantly reduced acuity—even with corrective lenses—to those who are blind. Depending on the nature and severity of their disability, children with visual impairments may need math materials with larger visual components or materials that are tactilely accessible. While the individual needs of children with visual impairments vary widely, many benefit from activities with enlarged visual images as well as materials that utilize other senses, such as touch or sound. While typically developing children often rely on visual images to help them create quantification relationships, children with visual impairments may make keener use of sound or tactile input to construct such relationships.

How can teachers design math materials to meet the needs of children with visual impairments?

Teachers can make visual images larger, transform two-dimensional images into three-dimensional ones, and utilize sounds to form mathematical sets. For some children, larger pictures on game boards and large dice are all that is needed to make math games accessible. Other children need materials that they can touch in order to process the information. Teachers can make math materials tactile by outlining images with puffy paint or cutting shapes out of felt or foam board rather than using stickers or stamp impressions. Puffy stickers used on dice enable children who cannot see flat dots to feel them. Tape recorded sounds allow all children, including those with visual impairments, to put quantities of sound into mathematical relationships rather than just relying on visual images for set comparisons. Activities 8.6 through 8.12 are designed for children with visual impairments.

How might a hearing impairment affect a child's use of math materials?

Children with hearing impairments may use math materials in much the same way as children who hear normally; however, they may need the teacher to help them communicate with other children about the rules of the game. Since children with hearing impairments can visualize sets, they use visual clues to help them quantify, as do typically developing children. However, some children with severe hearing impairments do not use spoken language. Thus, they may use fingers or sign language instead of counting words when they reach the counting stage of quantification.

Children with hearing impairments may hear sounds in a distorted way, hear sounds much softer than normal, or, in the case of Deaf children, have little residual hearing. This may alter the child's system of communication. In such cases, teachers can facilitate children's interactions when playing math games by using gestural clues to communicate turn-taking, rules, and observations of peers. For example, if a player thinks that a child with a hearing impairment moved too many spaces on a path game, the teacher might point to the child who made this observation, and then use fingers to indicate how many spaces the child says were moved when compared to the dice. The teacher might then shrug, in essence asking, "What do you think?" Teachers who know sign language may be able to translate for children who also sign.

How might children who have a diagnosis along the autism spectrum utilize math materials?

Autism spectrum is a broad diagnostic category encompassing a large range of communication-related difficulties, with autism being at the most severely impacted end of the continuum. Communication and processing problems may present obstacles to children in constructing mathematical relationships since typically these concepts develop within a social or communicative context. It is often difficult for teachers to assess how much a child with an autism spectrum disorder actually comprehends. Teachers may find that some children with this diagnosis require more time and concrete experiences in order to advance in mathematical thinking. Teachers may also find it more difficult to interest children with communication-related difficulties in math games and activities. When this is the case, teachers may wish to design math materials that are directly related to the interests and strengths of the individual child. Activities 8.13, 8.14, and 8.15 were designed to build on the skills of particular children with autism.

How can teachers modify math materials to meet the needs of children with autism spectrum disorders?

Teachers must reflect on the interests and communication strategies of the individual child and develop specific math activities based on those strengths. These activities may be very different from those developed for typically developing children or children with other types of disabilities. For example, if a child is only able to communicate the mathematical relationships of "more" and "no more," then that is the place to start when designing math activities for that child. Coordinating a math activity with a repetitive rhyme or book and integrating signing with math experiences are scaffolding strategies teachers may find effective with some children.

How might physical impairments affect a child's use of math materials?

Some children with physical impairments may be unable to successfully manipulate the pieces in math activities even though they may be mentally ready to create the mathematical relationships involved with the materials. Teachers or parents might erroneously infer that the child has a cognitive delay when the real problem is the child's inability to manipulate the materials. Teachers in these situations are challenged to design specific materials that maximize the child's capabilities.

How can teachers design math materials to meet the needs of children with physical impairments?

Teachers must analyze the specific strengths and difficulties of each child and develop new materials or modify existing ones accordingly. Some children with physical disabilities may need added physical support, such as a chair with arms, to give them the security to manipulate math materials. Other children may require larger dice, spinners, movers, and manipulative pieces in order to successfully play math games. Sometimes just taping the game board to the table may provide enough stability to enable a child with a physical impairment to play the game without frustration. Activities 8.3 and 8.5 incorporate larger manipulative pieces for children with motor delays.

Math Activities
for Inclusive Classrooms

8.1 Snow Friends
Cognitive Delays

Description

Very young children, or children with cognitive delays, may need additional opportunities to construct the concepts of one-to-one correspondence and quantification to two. For this activity, children can put one toy snowman and one toy person into each cardboard house. The houses can be easily made from half-pint milk cartons covered with contact paper. Readers who have made the doghouse game from *More Than Counting* (activity 2.10) can use the same houses.

Math Concepts

▲ one-to-one correspondence
▲ quantification to two

Materials

▲ 5 small wooden or plastic snowmen (large enough to not pose a choking hazard)
▲ 5 small plastic people, such as Duplo or Fisher-Price people
▲ 5 cardboard houses, made from half-pint milk cartons covered with contact paper

Child's Level

This activity is designed for preschool or kindergarten children with cognitive delays. Teachers may find that it also works well for toddlers or young preschoolers.

What to Look For

Some children will put one snowman and one person in each
house, especially if this is suggested as a possibility.

Some children will begin to quantify one and two objects,
especially after this has been modeled through play.

Children will play with the snowmen, people, and houses. It is
through such play that they begin to form mathematical relationships.

Modification

Once children have had many opportunities to put snowmen, people, and houses into mathematical relationships (such as one-to-
one correspondence), teachers may wish to introduce a spinner
divided into fourths, with a snowman or person sticker in each
section. Children can spin the spinner to determine whether to
place a person or a snowman into the house.

Comments and Questions to Extend Thinking

Can you put one snowman in each house?

Can you put one person in each house?

How many are in this house?

Can my person come to visit your house? Look! Now there
are two.

Can two snowmen play in this house?

Integrated Curriculum Activities

Introduce the board book version of *The Snowman,* by Raymond
Briggs (Boston: Little, Brown, 1985).

Use snowmen cookie cutters with playdough.

Sing simple snow songs (see *More Than Singing,* activities 2.6, 4.5,
and 6.6).

Recite the "5 Little Snowmen" poem (activity 5.5), but reduce the
number of snowmen to two.

Helpful Hints

Christmas tree orna-
ments are a good
source of wooden or
plastic snowmen. Be
sure they are nontoxic
and have no small
pieces that could pose a
choking hazard.

8.2 Snowflake Box
Cognitive Delays

Description

Children with cognitive or motor delays sometimes have trouble placing counters on grid boards in a one-to-one correspondence. This activity shows teachers how to modify a snowflake grid game by placing the same stickers in a clear plastic divided box instead of on a cardboard grid.

Math Concepts

▲ one-to-one correspondence
▲ quantification to two (optional)

Thanks to Nancy Struewing for this idea.

Materials

▲ 2 clear plastic divided boxes, each with 18 sections
▲ snowflake stickers
▲ 36 white pompoms (large enough not to pose a choking hazard)
▲ die, made from a 1-inch cube with one or two ¼-inch-round stickers per side (optional)

Child's Level

This game is designed for preschool or kindergarten children with cognitive delays. Teachers may find that it also works well with young preschoolers.

What to Look For

Children will put one pompom into each space in their box. Some children will want to fill and dump the box many times.

Modification

Introduce the teacher-made 1–2 die when you think the child may be ready. If the child is able to quantify to two, add a third dot to two sides of the die.

Comments and Questions to Extend Thinking

Can the pompoms go in this box?
Can you put one pompom in each space?
I need one more. Can you give me one?

Integrated Curriculum Activities

Put pompoms and jars in the sensory table with rice. Children can use spoons or tongs to pick up the pompoms and fill the jars.
Sing simple snow songs as you play the math game (see *More Than Singing,* activity 2.6).
Dramatize snowflakes falling (see *More Than Singing,* activity 6.6).

Helpful Hints

Look for the plastic boxes in craft stores. They are often used to hold embroidery floss.

8.3 Bottle Cap Cover-Up
Cognitive or Motor Delays

Description

This is another type of grid game modification for children with cognitive delays. As children move from divided boxes (activity 8.2) onto grid boards, they may need larger cover-up pieces. For this game, children hide the teddy bear stickers on a grid board by covering them with bottle caps. Children seem to enjoy the idea of hiding things. This game modification is also helpful for children with physical impairments who may have trouble picking up smaller counters.

Math Concepts

▲ one-to-one correspondence
▲ quantification to two (optional)

Materials

▲ 2 grid boards, made from poster board (10 by 5 inches), with 10 teddy bear stickers or stamped images arranged in 2 rows
▲ 20 milk bottle caps
▲ die, made from a 1-inch cube with one or two ¼-inch-round stickers on each side (optional)

Child's Level

This activity is designed for preschool or kindergarten children with cognitive delays. Teachers may find that it also works well with toddlers or young preschoolers.

What to Look For

Children will cover all of the bears by putting one bottle cap over each bear.

Some children will play peek-a-boo with the bears after they are covered.

Modification

After children are accustomed to covering the bears in one-to-one correspondence, the teacher may wish to add a simple, teacher-made die to introduce quantification. Limit the choices on the die to one or two dots at first.

Comments and Questions to Extend Thinking

Can you hide all of the teddy bears?
Can you uncover one bear?
Help me find two of my bears.

Integrated Curriculum Activities

Include more difficult teddy bear games for the rest of the class (see *More Than Counting*, activities 4.7, 5.3, and 5.14).
Read books about teddy bears, such as *When the Teddy Bears Came*, by Martin Waddell (Cambridge, MA: Candlewick, 1995).
Use teddy bear cookie cutters with playdough.

Helpful Hints

Plastic milk bottle caps are a good size to use for cover-up pieces. They are also colorful. Ask parents to help you collect them.

People Mover
Cognitive Delays

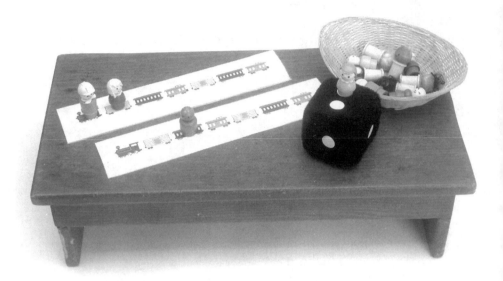

Description
Children with cognitive delays may spend more time in the quantification stage of one-to-one correspondence than typically developing children. They may try to place their counters on top of the dots on the die in order to see how many they need. The large die used in this activity allows children to set their people counters directly on the dots of the die before putting them into the cars on their train game boards.

Math Concepts
▲ one-to-one correspondence
▲ quantification
▲ creation of equivalent sets

Materials
▲ 1 large foam die, made by covering a 2-inch foam cube with felt pieces, whip-stitching around the edges, and adhering ½-inch felt circles to the die, with 1, 2, or 3 dots per side
▲ cylindrical toy people, such as Fisher-Price people or people made by gluing wooden beads onto wooden spools (be sure the heads cannot come off and pose a choking hazard)
▲ 2 train boards, made by adhering train stickers or cutouts to poster board pieces (13 by 3 inches) and laminating

Child's Level

While this game was designed for preschool or kindergarten children with cognitive delays, it is also popular with many typically developing preschoolers.

What to Look For

Many children will set their toy people directly on the dots of the large die before placing them in the train cars.

Many children will put one person in each car of their train.

Some children will try to quantify the number of people they have.

Some children will line the people up within the overall boundaries of the train, but not with one person per car. They are thinking globally and not yet in one-to-one correspondence.

Modifications

Some children may not yet be ready to compare sets using a die. For these children, eliminate the die at first so that they can focus on one-to-one correspondence by putting one person in each car on the train.

Large foam dice are available commercially once children are ready to quantify to six.

Comments and Questions to Extend Thinking

Can you win a person for each car on the train?

Choose a person for each circle on the die.

How many people do you need?

Integrated Curriculum Activities

Read books about trains, such as *Freight Train,* by Donald Crews (New York: Mulberry, 1978) and *Trains,* by Byron Barton (New York: Harper, 1986).

Transform the dramatic play area into a train. Just lining up the chairs in a row often suggests a train to children.

Sing train songs (see *More Than Singing,* activity 6.12).

A hot glue gun works well for gluing the head to the spool base when making spool people. A dowel inserted through the spool and head helps hold them together.

Check automotive departments for dashboard dice when children are ready for a 1–6 die.

8.5 Pirate Game–Bigger Jewels
Cognitive Delays or Physical Impairments

Description

This modification makes the "Pirate Treasure" game (activity 6.3) accessible for children with cognitive or motor delays. Larger jewels, which are easier to manipulate, replace the smaller jewels in the original activity, and a 1–3 die is substituted for the 1–6 die for children who are not yet ready to deal with quantities larger than three. This activity demonstrates how easy it often is to modify existing activities for children with disabilities.

Math Concepts

▲ one-to-one correspondence
▲ creation and comparison of sets
▲ quantification

Materials

▲ 2 grid boards, made from black poster board (10 by 4 inches), and 14 pirate stickers (see activity 6.3 for a more complete description)
▲ 28 large plastic "jewels," approximately 1 by ½ inch
▲ a 1–3 die, made from a 1-inch cube with one, two, or three ¼-inch round stickers on each side

Child's Level

This activity is designed to meet the needs of preschool or kindergarten children with cognitive or motor delays, but it is also suitable for typically developing preschoolers.

What to Look For

Children with motor delays will find it easier to manipulate the large jewels than small jewels or marble chips.

Many children will place one jewel on each sticker in one-to-one correspondence.

Some children will roll the die and attempt to take an equivalent number of jewels.

Some children will quantify the number of dots on the die and the number of jewels they take.

Modification

For children who have trouble quantifying to three, substitute a die with only one or two dots per side.

Questions to Extend Thinking

Can you collect a jewel for each pirate?

How many jewels should I take?

Does every pirate have a jewel?

Integrated Curriculum Activities

Read the book *Tough Boris,* by Mem Fox (New York: Harcourt, 1994).

Design pirate board games for the class (activities 6.3, 7.3a, and 7.3b).

Put glitter and sequins on the art shelf for gluing.

Look for the large jewels in craft supply stores. For children who still put objects in their mouths, be sure to use counters that will not pose a choking hazard.

8.6 3-D Heart Game
Visual Impairments

Description

This activity is a modification of a heart grid game for children
with visual impairments. The heart shapes on the grid boards are
raised stickers instead of flat ones, and the die has raised dots.
This allows children who have trouble seeing shapes on a flat surface to feel them. Typically developing children find the game
equally attractive and interesting.

Math Concepts

▲ one-to-one correspondence
▲ creation and comparison of sets
▲ quantification

Materials

▲ 2 grid boards, made from white poster board (6 by 6 inches)
   with 9 puffy heart stickers on each board
▲ heart links, to use as counters that fit over the puffy stickers
▲ a 1–4 die, made from a 1-inch cube, with sets of 1 to 4 small
   puffy heart stickers on each side

Child's Level

This activity is appropriate for either preschool or kindergarten
children, *including* children with visual disabilities.

What to Look For

Children will roll the die to determine how many heart links to place on their grid boards.

Children with visual impairments may feel the puffy dots on the die and grid board to determine how many heart links to take and where to place them.

Children will use a quantification strategy (global, one-to-one correspondence, or counting) commensurate with their level of thinking.

Some children will quantify the number of heart links they have on their board.

Modification

If four is too large a number for a particular child or group of children to quantify, switch to a 1–3 die, also made with puffy stickers.

Questions to Extend Thinking

How many dots do you feel on the die?
Can you find as many hearts as you have dots on the die?
Can you feel spaces where you can put the heart links?
Are there any stickers left that don't have heart links?

Integrated Curriculum Activities

Put heart shapes cut from a variety of materials on the art shelf.
Use heart-shaped cookie cutters with playdough.
Clap the word for *friend* in other languages as a rhythm activity (see *More Than Singing,* activity 3.3).

Helpful Hints

Curtain rings can be substituted for heart links if the heart links are hard to find.

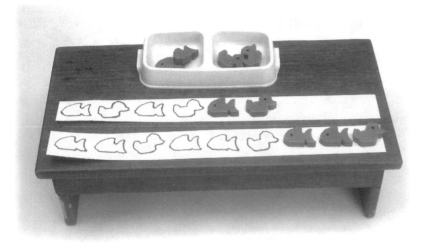

8.7 Animal Patterns
Visual Impairments

Description

This activity demonstrates an easy way to modify a patterning activity to make it accessible to children with visual impairments. Fish and duck shapes are traced onto cardboard strips from plastic cookie cutters to form various patterns. Then the shapes are outlined with puffy paint. When the paint dries, children can feel the shapes as well as see them. They can then use the cookie cutters to reproduce the patterns or create their own. Many patterning activities or game boards can be modified in the same way for classes that include a child with a visual disability. The alteration does not make the material any less attractive or less interesting to the rest of the class.

Math Concepts

▲ patterning
▲ similarities and differences

Materials

▲ pattern strips, made from poster board, with animal shapes outlined in puffy paint and arranged to form patterns:
  fish–duck, fish–duck
  fish–fish–duck, fish–fish–duck
  duck–duck–fish–fish, duck–duck–fish–fish
▲ animal cookie cutters that match the shapes on the pattern strips

Child's Level

This activity is appropriate for preschool or kindergarten children and also meets the needs of children with visual impairments.

What to Look For

Children will look at the pattern strips or feel them to distinguish the pattern.

Children will use the cookie cutters to re-create the patterns on the pattern strips.

Some children will have difficulty distinguishing the patterns and may benefit from having the patterns chanted rhythmically (see chapter 2).

Some children will create their own patterns.

Modification

Create longer and more complex patterns once the children have constructed the concept of patterns with the easier pattern strips. More shapes can be introduced, as well as longer strands that repeat:

> duck–fish–snail, duck–fish–snail
> duck–duck–fish–snail, duck–duck–fish–snail

Questions to Extend Thinking

Can you feel the shapes of these animals?

What order are the animals in?

What animal should come next?

Can you make the pattern with these cookie cutters?

Integrated Curriculum Activities

Use the animal cookie cutters with playdough. Some children may create patterns with the playdough shapes.

Bake animal cookies.

Include animal-shape puzzles in the manipulative area.

Add plastic animals to the block area.

Helpful Hints

Glue from squeeze bottles can also be used to outline the shapes.

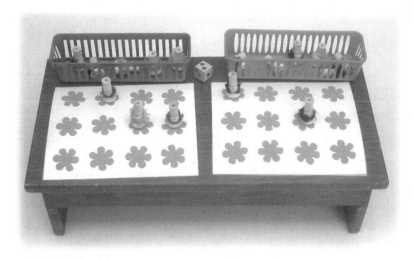

8.8 Upside-Down Grid–Modification
Visual Impairments

Description

This game is a modification of the "Walking Upside Down" grid game (activity 6.1) inspired by the book *Silly Sally,* by Audrey Wood. Raised flowers cut from colorful foam board form the spaces of the grid boards. This enables children with visual impairments to feel the spaces on their game. The upside-down spool people that are used for the counters are the same as in activity 5.14. Plastic flower shapes could also be used.

Math Concepts

▲ one-to-one correspondence
▲ creation and comparison of sets
▲ quantification

Materials

▲ 2 grid boards, made from poster board (8 by 5 inches), with 12 flower shapes cut from pastel foam board and glued to each poster board to form the grids
▲ 24 spool people, each made by gluing together doll hair, a macramé bead head, and a wooden spool and mounting it upside down on a wooden disk
▲ a 1–6 die, made by gluing puffy stickers to a 1-inch cube in sets from 1 to 6

Child's Level

This activity is appropriate for preschool and kindergarten children, including children with visual disabilities.

What to Look For

Children will roll the die to determine how many upside-down people to place on their grid boards.

Children with visual impairments may feel the puffy dots on the die and the raised flowers on the grid board to determine how many upside-down people to take and where to place them.

Children will use a quantification strategy (global, one-to-one correspondence, or counting) commensurate with their level of thinking.

Some children will quantify the number of upside-down people they have on their board.

Modification

If six is too large a number for a particular child or group of children to quantify, switch to a 1–3 die, also made with puffy stickers.

Questions to Extend Thinking

How many dots do you feel on the die?
Can you find as many people as you have dots on the die?
Can you feel spaces where you can put the people?
Can you set the people upside down?
Are there any flowers left that don't have people?

Integrated Curriculum Activities

Read *Silly Sally*, by Audrey Wood (New York: Harcourt, 1992) to the class.

Do wheelbarrow walks with the children outside or in the gross-motor room. The teacher holds the children's feet so that they can walk on their hands upside-down like Silly Sally.

Include *Silly Sally* word cards with the names of the characters from the book in the writing area. The words can be traced with puffy paint so that children with visual impairments can feel them, or the words can be punched out with a Braille writer.

Let children dramatize *Silly Sally* as you read the book.

Helpful Hints

Foam board is available in craft stores. Felt can also be used.

8.9 Farm Parade—Tactile
Visual Impairments

Thanks to Lisa Heintz for the use of this game.

Description

This game is an adaptation of a farm path game for children with visual impairments. The paths on the game board are delineated with raised shapes so that children who have difficulty seeing the paths can feel them. A section of plastic fence glued to the game board designates the end of the paths and can also be felt. The game board is attractive and colorful and therefore appeals to typically developing children as well as children with special needs. This activity coordinates well with the books *I Went Walking,* by Sue Williams, and *The Boy with a Drum,* by David L. Harrison.

Math Concepts

▲ creation and comparison of sets
▲ quantification
▲ one-to-one correspondence

Materials

▲ game board (as pictured), made from white poster board (22 by 16 inches) with felt triangles, metallic circles, and rectangular Velcro for the 3 paths
▲ small plastic farm animals for movers
▲ a 1–3 die, made by gluing puffy stickers to a 1-inch cube in sets from 1 to 3

Child's Level

This activity is appropriate for preschool and kindergarten children, including children with visual disabilities.

What to Look For

Children will move the farm animals along the path to reach the fence.

Children who have trouble seeing the path will feel it to know where to move.

Many children will use the die to determine how many spaces to move.

Children with visual disabilities may feel the die to determine how many spaces to move.

Some children will hop along the path without regard to the number on the die. Teachers can model quantification strategies when it is their turn.

Modification

Make a long path version of the game, also with a raised path, once children are successful with the short path game. Switch to a 1–6 tactile die or two tactile dice.

Questions to Extend Thinking

How can you tell where to move your animal?

Can you feel how many bumps are on the die?

Can you move your animal as many spaces on your path as there are bumps on the die?

How many more spaces can you feel before you reach the fence?

Integrated Curriculum Activities

Read *I Went Walking,* by Sue Williams (New York: Harcourt, 1989) and *The Boy with a Drum,* by David L. Harrison (New York: Golden, 1971) to the class.

Put animal word cards in the writing area. The names of the animals can be traced with puffy paint so children can feel them, or they can be punched out with a Braille writer.

Make patterns with farm animal cookie cutters (see activity 8.7).

Clap farm animal names for a rhythm activity (see *More Than Singing,* chapter 3).

Helpful Hints

Look for animals that match the ones in either of the books listed. Then children can re-create the story as they play the game.

8.10 Baby Owl Tactile Path Game

Visual Impairments

Description

This activity shows teachers a simple way to alter existing path games to meet the needs of children with visual impairments. It is a modification of the "Baby Owls" long path game (activity 7.2b). The spaces on the path are outlined with silver puffy paint so that children who have difficulty seeing the path can feel it. One or two dice with raised stickers replace the standard dice used in the original game. The owl movers are mounted on wooden pieces of different shapes so that children can distinguish their movers either visually or by feeling them.

Math Concepts

▲ creation and comparison of sets
▲ quantification
▲ one-to-one correspondence
▲ addition

Materials

▲ game board, as described in activity 7.2b, with the path spaces outlined in silver puffy paint
▲ owl movers, mounted on wooden disks of various shapes, such as a circle, triangle, or square
▲ one or two 1–6 dice, made by gluing puffy stickers to 2-inch cubes in sets from 1 to 6

Child's Level

This activity is appropriate for older preschool and kindergarten children, including children with visual disabilities.

What to Look For

Children who have trouble seeing the path will feel it to know
where to move.

Many children will use the dice to determine how many spaces
to move.

Children with visual disabilities may feel the dice to determine
how many spaces to move.

Some children will add the dice together by counting all the dots.

Some children will move their owls along the path without regard
to the number on the dice. Teachers can model quantification
strategies when it is their turn.

Modification

If this long path game is too difficult, try modifying the "Baby
Owls" short path game (activity 7.2a) in the same way. Switch to a
single 1–3 die made with puffy stickers.

Questions to Extend Thinking

How can you tell where to move your owl?

Can you feel how many bumps are on the dice?

Can you feel as many spaces on your path as there are bumps on
the dice?

How many more spaces can you feel before you catch up to
Maria's owl?

Integrated Curriculum Activities

Read the book *Owl Babies,* by Martin Waddell (Cambridge, MA:
Candlewick, 1992) to the class.

Put word cards with the names of the characters from *Owl Babies*
in the writing center. The words can be traced with puffy paint
so that children with visual impairments can feel them, or they
can be punched out with a Braille writer.

Let children dramatize owls perching on branches, flapping their
wings, and flying.

Include a bird math manipulative game in the math area (activity
5.10).

Helpful Hints

Look for wood shapes to
mount the owl movers
on in craft stores or with
collage materials in
catalogs.

8.11 Baby Grid Sound Game
Visual Impairments

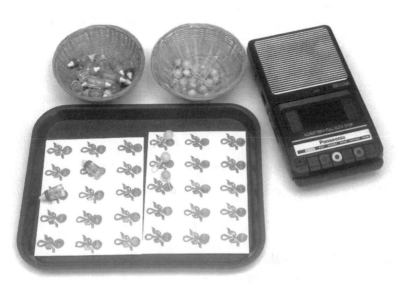

Description
This game focuses on sound rather than sight as the medium used to delineate mathematical sets. It is a modification of a baby grid game, such as activity 6.9. The grid consists of rubber stamp impressions of baby rattles mounted on poster board and outlined with puffy paint so that they can be felt by children with visual impairments. Instead of rolling a die or spinning a spinner, players activate a tape recording of sounds to determine the quantity and type of counters to take on each turn. The counters are tiny novelty baby bottles or rattles. For each turn, the player turns on the tape recorder and hears the sound of either a rattle or a baby crying "wah." If the sound is a rattle, the child takes as many toy rattles as rattle sounds on the tape recording and places them on the grid board. If the sound is a baby crying, an equivalent number of baby bottles can be taken. This game is stimulating to typically developing children as well as children with disabilities since it requires them to form mathematical relationships involving sets of sounds instead of sets they can see.

Math Concepts
▲ creation and comparison of sets
▲ quantification
▲ one-to-one correspondence

Materials
▲ 2 grid boards, made from white poster board (8 by 6 inches), with 15 stamped impressions of baby rattles outlined with puffy paint on each board to form the grids
▲ tape recording of a random series of from 1 to 4 sounds of rattles or baby cries ("wah"), with a recorded direction of "stop" at the end of each set of sounds
▲ 30 small novelty baby bottles
▲ 30 small novelty baby rattles

Child's Level

This activity is appropriate for older preschool and kindergarten children, including children with visual disabilities.

What to Look For

Children will listen to the tape to determine how many rattles or baby bottles to take.

Some children will take a bottle or rattle each time they hear a sound; other children will count the sounds and then count the rattles or bottles as they take them.

Some children will put one bottle or rattle on each sticker on their grid boards.

Some children will put a rattle and a bottle on each space.

Some children will quantify the number of bottles and rattles they have at the end of the game.

Modification

If using two different kinds of counters is confusing for some children, start with just one type of sound on the tape and one type of counter.

Questions to Extend Thinking

Can you find the basket of rattles and the basket of baby bottles?
Can you take one rattle for each rattle sound on the tape?
How do you know how many bottles to take?
How many spaces are left to fill on your board?

Integrated Curriculum Activities

Sing songs about babies with the children (see *More Than Singing,* activities 2.9, 2.12, and 2.13).

Make a matching game with baby stickers. Outline the stickers with puffy paint so that children with visual disabilities can feel them.

Adapt other types of baby games (activities 7.9a and 7.9b) for use with children with disabilities.

Let the children make baby cereal and taste baby food.

Put a variety of types of rattles in the music area for experimentation (see *More Than Magnets,* activity 6.13).

At first children may need some assistance with operating the tape recorder. Put a raised shape on the start button and a different shape on the stop button so that children with visual impairments can feel them. Felt works well.

8.12 Alligator Purse Sound Game
Visual Impairments

Description

This game, which correlates with the popular children's song "The Lady with the Alligator Purse," is an adaptation of an alligator long path game. The dice are replaced by a tape recording of sounds that determine how many spaces players can move on each turn. The spaces on the path are made with circles cut from felt so that children with visual impairments can feel them. Typically developing children are also intrigued with the tape recording and enjoy playing the game.

Math Concepts

▲ creation and comparison of sets
▲ quantification
▲ one-to-one correspondence

Materials

▲ game board, made from gold poster board (22 by 17 inches), with dark green ¾-inch round self-adhesive felt circles to delineate the path
▲ alligator shape cut from green felt, glued to the board for the start space
▲ 1½-inch brown felt circle, decorated to look like pizza, glued to the board for the end space

Helpful Hints

At first children may need some assistance with operating the tape recorder. Put a raised shape on the start button and a different shape on the stop button so that children with visual impairments can feel them. Felt works well.

▲ tape recording of a random series of from 1 to 4 sounds played on a triangle, with a recorded direction of "stop" at the end of each set of sounds

▲ small alligator movers, each with a different felt shape glued to its back, so that children can identify their movers by sight or touch

Child's Level

This activity is appropriate for older preschool and kindergarten children, including children with visual disabilities.

What to Look For

Children will listen to the sounds on the tape recording to determine how many spaces to move along the path.

Some children will move one space along the path each time they hear a sound; other children will first count the sounds and then attempt to move the same number of spaces along the path.

Children who have trouble seeing the path will feel the spaces in order to know where to move.

Some children will move their alligators along the path without regard to the number of sounds they hear. Teachers can model quantification strategies when it is their turn.

Modification

Increase the number of sounds on the tape recorder for children who can easily make equivalent sets to four.

Questions to Extend Thinking

Can you move one space for each sound you hear?

How many spaces should I move my alligator?

How many more spaces do you need to move to get to the end of the path?

Integrated Curriculum Activities

Read and sing a book version of *The Lady with the Alligator Purse,* such as the one by Nadine Bernard Westcott (Boston: Little, Brown, 1988).

Put a pizza parlor or doctor's office in the dramatic play area.

8.13 "More" Game
Autism Spectrum Disorders

Description

Teachers often find it challenging to help children with severe language limitations to progress in the formation of mathematical concepts. However, some children who do not use spoken language are able to use signs. The sign for "more" is often one of the first to emerge. This game piggybacks beginning quantification skills onto the ability to sign "more." Children play by spinning a spinner divided in half, with one visual symbol for "more" on one half of the spinner and two symbols for "more" on the other half. Children can select one or two counters (in this case, small dinosaurs) to correspond to the quantity on the spinner. Teachers help by modeling the sign for "more" and pairing it with a dinosaur.

Math Concepts
▲ one-to-one correspondence
▲ quantification of one and two

Materials
▲ teacher-made spinner, as pictured and described above
▲ counters that appeal to the child (in this case, dinosaurs)

Child's Level
This game is appropriate for preschool and kindergarten children with severe language limitations.

What to Look For

Some children with autism spectrum disorders may require many experiences with this and similar games before they begin to construct the relationship between the number of times "more" is signed and the number of objects they can take.

Many children will need adult facilitation to model the sign for "more" appropriately in the context of the game.

Modification

If the intended child is too distracted by the spinner, eliminate the spinner and take turns signing "more" and taking one dinosaur.

Questions to Extend Thinking

Can you take one more? (Say this while pointing to the picture on the spinner and signing "more.")

Can you take two more? (Say this while pointing to each of the two "more" signs on the appropriate side of the spinner, one at a time, and signing "more" each time a picture is pointed to.)

Integrated Curriculum Activities

Model signing "more" one or two times and then giving a corresponding number of pieces of food at snack or lunch.

Model signing "more" one or two times and then giving a corresponding number of toys or blocks whenever appropriate during the day.

Helpful Hints

Photocopy the visual representation of "more" to use on the spinner.

8.14 Owl Flannel Board– 1, 2, and a Lot!
Autism Spectrum Disorders

Description

This activity was originally designed for a child with autism, but it is also appropriate for children with language or cognitive delays. It is based on the book *Good-Night Owl,* by Pat Hutchins, which is popular with many young children and was a favorite of the child for whom the original activity was created. It involves quantifying one, two, or "a lot" as children find the appropriate number of flannel board characters to match the characters in the book.

Math Concepts

▲ one-to-one correspondence
▲ quantification of one, two, and "a lot"

Materials

▲ flannel board pieces to match the characters in the book, made by cutting the pieces from felt and gluing them together
▲ flannel board
▲ copy of *Good-Night Owl* to keep next to the activity

Child's Level

This game is appropriate for preschool and kindergarten children with severe language limitations or cognitive delays. Typically developing children also enjoy it.

What to Look For

Children will look for the flannel board pieces to correspond to the characters on each page of the book.

Children will begin to notice that there is only one owl, squirrel, woodpecker, cuckoo, and robin, but there are two crows, doves, jays, and starlings. There are lots of sparrows and bees.

Modification

None suggested.

Comments and Questions to Extend Thinking

How many squirrels do you see?

Can you find the doves?

We need one crow for this picture and one crow for this picture—one, two.

Look at all the bees! There are a lot.

Integrated Curriculum Activities

Include *Good-Night Owl,* by Pat Hutchins (New York: Macmillan, 1972) in the reading area, and read the big book version of it to the class. Put bird nests in the science area.

Sing simple bird songs (see *More Than Singing,* activity 2.2).

Include other stories about owls, such as *Owl Babies,* by Martin Waddell (Cambridge, MA: Candlewick, 1992), in the book area.

Helpful Hints

Be sure you have the correct number of flannel board pieces to correspond to the number of each character in the book. The number of bees is not important, but you'll probably want at least five.

8.15 Cookie Jar Game
Autism Spectrum Disorders

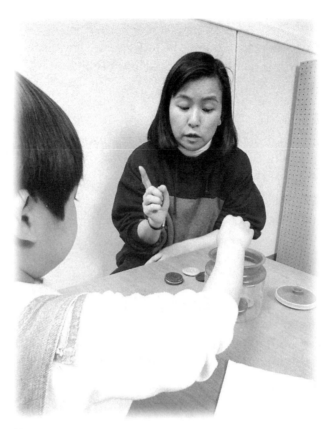

Description
This is a quantification game designed for children with autism spectrum disorders or severe language delays. Children may respond to the repetitive words of the chant and enjoy adding one cookie at a time to the cookie jar. It is a variation of the familiar children's chant "Who Took the Cookie."

> Who put *one* cookie in the cookie jar?
> *(Child's name)* put *one* cookie in the cookie jar.
>
> Who put *two* cookies in the cookie jar?
> *(Child's name)* put *two* cookies in the cookie jar.

Math Concepts
▲ one-to-one correspondence
▲ quantification of one and two

Materials

▲ plastic cookie jar
▲ plastic cookies

Child's Level

This game is appropriate for preschool and kindergarten children with severe language limitations or cognitive delays. Typically developing children also enjoy it.

What to Look For

Children will take turns putting one or two cookies in the cookie jar as they repeat the chant with the teacher.

Modification

Once the children become adept at adding one or two cookies to the jar, increase the number used in the chant to three and then four.

Comments and Questions to Extend Thinking

I see one cookie going into the cookie jar!
Two cookies—one for each hand.

Integrated Curriculum Activities

Add magnetic cookies and a gridded cookie sheet to the dramatic
  play area (see activity 1.1).
Bake cookies with the children.
Read *The Doorbell Rang,* by Pat Hutchins (New York: Greenwillow,
  1986), which also has repetitive words and deals with cookies.

Helpful Hints

Print the words to the chant on a chart. Children can add their names to the chart.

Appendix

Terms and Definitions for Assessment Forms

term	definition	example
free play	Imaginative play, not necessarily involving math	A child hops the squirrel counters randomly around the grid board and pretends they are collecting nuts.
makes sets	Attempts to construct sets of a particular quantity	A child rolls the die and takes the same number of counters as dots on the die or moves the same number of spaces along a path.
global	Takes a handful, or fills in randomly within boundaries	A child rolls the die and then grabs a handful of counters.
1:1	Uses one-to-one correspondence to take an equivalent amount	A child takes a game piece each time she points to a dot on the die or places one counter on each sticker of a grid game.
counts	Uses counting to decide how many to take	A child counts the dots on the die and then counts a corresponding number of game pieces or moves a corresponding number of spaces along a path.
stable-order	Says the number words in the correct order	A child counts 1, 2, 3, 4 in the same order each time. After 4, the number words vary: 1, 2, 3, 4, 8, 6; 1, 2, 3, 4, 6, 9; 1, 2, 3, 4, 9, 8.
skips	Skips over some objects when counting	A child points to the stars faster than she counts. * * * * * * * 1 2 3 4 5
re-counts	Counts some objects more than once	A child counts the stars in the first row, then the stars in the second row, and then some from the first row again.
counts all	Combines two dice by counting all the dots	A child counts all the dots on one die and continues counting all the dots on a second die.
adds on	Knows quantity of first set and counts on without re-counting the first set	A child rolls a three and a six. Recognizing the three, she counts on: 4, 5, 6, 7, 8, 9.
combinations	Remembers some addition combinations	Most children remember "doubles" first, for example, 1 + 1 = 2; 2 + 2 = 4; 3 + 3 = 6.

Individual Assessment Form

Child:

date	material	outcome		strategy			errors			addition			comments
		free play	makes sets	global	1:1	counts	stable-order to	skips	re-counts	counts all	adds on	knows comb.	

More Than Counting